Black Religion / Womanist Thought / Social Justice
Series Editors Dwight N. Hopkins and Linda E. Thomas
Published by Palgrave Macmillan

# Religio-Political Narratives in the United States

## From Martin Luther King, Jr. to Jeremiah Wright

*Angela D. Sims, F. Douglas Powe Jr., and
Johnny Bernard Hill*

RELIGIO-POLITICAL NARRATIVES IN THE UNITED STATES
Copyright © Angela D. Sims, F. Douglas Powe Jr., and
Johnny Bernard Hill, 2014.

First published in 2014 by
PALGRAVE MACMILLAN®
in the United States—a division of St. Martin's Press LLC,
175 Fifth Avenue, New York, NY 10010.

Where this book is distributed in the UK, Europe and the rest of the world,
this is by Palgrave Macmillan, a division of Macmillan Publishers Limited,
registered in England, company number 785998, of Houndmills,
Basingstoke, Hampshire RG21 6XS.

Palgrave Macmillan is the global academic imprint of the above companies
and has companies and representatives throughout the world.

Palgrave® and Macmillan® are registered trademarks in the United States,
the United Kingdom, Europe and other countries.

ISBN: 978–0–230–10956–8

Library of Congress Cataloging-in-Publication Data

Sims, Angela D.
    Religio-political narratives in the United States : from Martin Luther
King Jr. to Jeremiah Wright / Angela D. Sims, F. Douglas Powe Jr., and
Johnny Bernard Hill.
        pages cm.—(Black religion, womanist thought, social justice)
    Includes bibliographical references and index.
    ISBN 978–0–230–10956–8 (alk. paper)
    1. African Americans —Religion. 2. Black theology. 3. African American
churches. 4. Christianity and politics —United States. 5. Church and
state—United States. 6. Race relations —Religious aspects —Christianity.
    I. Title.

BR563.N4S56 2014
277.3'08208996073—dc23                                    2014000724

A catalogue record of the book is available from the British Library.

Design by Newgen Knowledge Works (P) Ltd., Chennai, India.

First edition: June 2014

10 9 8 7 6 5 4 3 2 1

To Katie Geneva Cannon who encourages me always to
follow my questions (ads)

To my seminary companions who helped to
shape my thinking (fdp)

To the voiceless and all who suffer (jbh)

# Contents

# Preface

In March 2008, media networks aired sound bites from Jeremiah Wright's April 13, 2003, sermon "Confusing God and Government," wherein Wright declared that God and the United States of America are not synonymous. Described by many journalists as incendiary and divisive, the recordings, which received nonstop replay, led to questions about the black church, black prophetic preaching, black theology, and patriotism. Historians and scholars in various disciplines have documented the long tradition of the black church and black prophetic preaching in the United States. Theologian James Cone, the progenitor of black theology, and other scholars of religion continue to stress that we cannot ignore the relationship between context and the manner in which we envision God. Yet, responses to excerpts from the above-mentioned sermon led to a further widening of the racial divide in the United States. A dynamic tension emerged, and it continues to be a point of contention. Some viewed Wright as anti-white and thus anti-American, yet, on the other hand, others recognized his social-ethical analysis as prophetic. Given that racial divides are endemic to life in the United States, we must attend to an underlying narrative that symbolizes the uniqueness of this particular situation.

For the first time in United States history, an African American male is now in his second term as the forty-fourth president of this nation. In 2008, at the center of the controversy surrounding Wright's sermon was then Senator Barack Hussein Obama, the presumptive presidential nominee of the Democratic Party. He was a member of Trinity United Church of Christ in Chicago where Jeremiah Wright was the pastor. At the time that Wright began to receive increased media attention, some inferred that Obama was, like his now former pastor, anti-white. At the same time, others, who believed that Obama was shaped or at least influenced by Wright's ministry, purported that he was better prepared to navigate the racial divide in the United States. Irrespective of their stance, both sides focused on Wright's ability to affect Obama's viewpoint and in so doing ignored narratives that form Wright's ministry.

Wright's social-cultural analysis is a response to a religious narrative in which he argues for the separation of church and state with specific attention to the way in which certain Christian themes, such as grace and justice, function. For example, God bless America is a simple phrase that many politicians use to convey their Christian and political beliefs to the public. While there are many ways to interpret this phrase, emphasis is often placed on a patriotic reassurance that the United States is and should be blessed by God. This position assumes and promotes a myth that the United States is a theocracy. As such, we posit that a problem with Wright's sermon, "Confusing God and Government," was his audacity to call into question another aspect of this country's religious and political narrative. At stake is whether Wright's theological ethical analysis of the United States' religious and political narrative is unpatriotic rhetoric. Wright's ability to offer an informed historical critique emerges from and is informed by a theological claim that one can be "unashamedly black and unapologetically Christian"[1] calls into question an often assumed, unquestioned, unarticulated, universal view of Christianity that is synonymous with white culture.[2]

Interestingly, Wright has preached many similar sermons throughout his more than 30-year ministry. Informed by a biblical text and world events, he addressed issues that most clergy tend to ignore to throngs at black ecclesial and educational institutions, and social and church organizations in Brazil and West Africa. Yet, he did not become a household name in the United States until Obama became a front-runner for the Democratic presidential nomination.

Since the national media was not concerned with Wright before 2008, can we assume that if Obama were not part of the equation that Wright would not receive the attention granted to him during the 2008 presidential campaign? Is it also possible to conclude, though we do not address this explicitly, that non-sustained media attention to Willard Mitt Romney's, the 2012 Republican presidential candidate, religious worldview, which many protestant religious spokespersons characterized as a cult during the 2008 campaign, is in some way overridden by ideations of whiteness? After all, Billy Graham, a renowned evangelical leader in the United States, "removed Mormonism from a list of "cults" on his website after handing his endorsement to GOP candidate Mitt Romney. This action privileged race and sufficed as evidence to satisfy concerns as Romney's white evangelical supporters sought to "stay away from a highly contentious issue."[3] Unlike Obama, Romney is a leader in his church and was able to avoid discussing his religious views. A leader in the Church of Jesus Christ of Latter Day Saints, Romney did, on occasion, "talk about the practices of his faith, but not the doctrines of his religion"[4] not even a 1978 change that made the priesthood available to all worthy males regardless of race.[5]

How then, are we to interpret the media portrayals of Wright's depiction of the United States? In a land where citizens self-identify as democratic, and where freedom of speech is viewed as a sacred cultural value, in what way was the 2008 controversy more about Wright's audacity to articulate an alternative interpretation of this nation's religious and political narrative than the tenor and flavor of his sermonic delivery? Could it be that Wright's opponents were fearful and his proponents were hopeful that he called into question how the religiopolitical narrative of this country would be viewed not only by Americans but also by the world?

Wright, a military veteran, is not the first African American preacher who openly opposed the United States' involvement in a war. Martin Luther King, Jr.'s opposition to this country's engagement in Viet Nam marked a change in his theology. Yet, with rare exception, analyses of prophetic discourse within the African American tradition do not highlight this shift in King's religious formation. Is it possible that focus on "a dream" without adequate attention to factors that inform this ideal, contribute to a sterilized nonthreatening depiction of King that stands in stark contrast to a vocal in-your-face Wright? After all, a striking difference between Wright and King is the tendency to remember King more for his prophetic role in leading nonviolent demonstrations during the 1960s rather than his stance against a conflict that was never officially declared a war by the United States Congress. However, one of his famous speeches, delivered at Riverside Church in New York City exactly one year prior to his assassination, is entitled, "Why I Am Opposed to the War in Viet Nam." Today, King's opposition to the war tends to get downplayed, but at the time of his response to the United States' engagement in the armed conflict, his popularity began to wane because he was perceived by some as unpatriotic.

This prompts us to consider what patriotism is and who determines whether one is deemed to have conformed or deviated from the established standard. At the same time, it is imperative that we construct a working definition of prophetic in order to determine how it functions in our contemporary world. In addition, we must examine how, or if, race shapes conversations about national devotion when sacred and secular interpretations emerge in the public sphere that challenge an underlying religiopolitical narrative of the United States that presents God and country as synonymous. In this book, we examine various political themes in selected sermons by King and Wright as well as provide biographical snapshots of several preachers as a way to place King and Wright within a larger tradition of the US jeremiad, which rhetorically calls the nation to account while simultaneously situating the ministers within the black church tradition.

We present evidence to refute a universal concept of the underlying narrative in United States culture characterized by life, liberty, and the pursuit of happiness. At issue is an understanding that accounts for existential realities of persons across racial, gender, and class lines that shape interpretations of this narrative. Accordingly, some can, like Rush Limbaugh, say, "I hope President Obama fails," because he interprets the

US narrative in a way that defines life, liberty, and the pursuit of happiness from a perspective of modernity and contract theory. At the same time, others, including President Obama, can interpret the same narrative from a postmodern perspective that is more communal and moves toward reclaiming an idea of the common good. These two ways of interpreting this country's narrative, while not dialectically opposed, are contentious and call on us to embody the story in different ways. If Obama's narrative succeeds, those who support Limbaugh's version of the modern project fear a new narrative that is more inclusive and undermines individualistic notions of wholeness. Even as we write, this perspective continues to have dire consequences for a large and growing population of the United States as Congress enacts legislation that erodes this country's safety net.

Following this line of thinking, we explain that reproductions of bigotry and associated theological ethical implications are inseparable from methods employed by language brokers who are adept in their ability to employ discourse skillfully to promote a monolithic portrayal of the United States by "any means necessary." We illustrate how language can be used as a foil to disguise racial hatred. We draw upon the writings of numerous scholars to substantiate our claim that discourse, in the form of racialized language, continues to play a central role in the study of prejudice, discrimination, and racism. In many respects the manner in which language is employed as a symbol to express, signal, confirm, describe, legitimate, or enact ethnic dominance is often viewed simultaneously by some to depict representations of God and the United States as synonymous. A risk associated with this tendency to conflate the Divine with all things America is a perpetuation of an interlocking cycle of oppression by select individuals who, because of access to public modes of communication, use points of privilege and access to distort representations of truth. It is little wonder then that, given practices of racial hatred in the United States, most whites do not usually admit such discriminatory practices to other whites, at least not in official contexts of inquiry. Consequently, social cognitions of white group members about minorities contribute to maintaining a social framework that supports discriminatory actions, often masked as national loyalty.

Counter to claims that suggest otherwise, we assert we do not live in a color blind nor "a racialized" society. President Obama is mixed! President Obama is black! President Obama is not really American because his dad was African. These and similar phrases, uttered initially during the 2008 presidential campaign, demonstrate the extent to which some will go in an effort to define President Obama's heritage, patriotism, and stances on things black. The real issue for many is not Obama's heritage, but how black is he. Is he King black or Malcolm X black? Many of his supporters worked hard in 2008 to color him in the image of King. Many of his detractors worked hard to connect him to Rev. Jeremiah Wright and to shade him as Malcolm X black. In the twenty-first century, even as many of us celebrate an African American president, this question of blackness continues to haunt the United States of America.

Is there a real difference in blackness? If so, who determines how we define blackness? These were not only questions pressed by Anglo Americans during the 2008 election but are also questions raised consistently within African American communities. A challenge is whether we can maintain historical ideas about blackness as we move forward and develop new theological insights about blackness that navigate either/or distinctions.

In response to these questions, we reflect on ways in which the deep roots of a prophetic Christian heritage point to hope and justice as key themes throughout history, and serve as a resource to assess intersections of US politics and religion today. These themes also offer alternative visions for religious and political discourse in the United States that seems to have received much media attention in recent years. We argue that prophetic dimensions of Christianity provide an important way forward as we navigate the complex terrain of religious conflict, and the problem of technology and information in our current age. We assert this view as an essential perspective that holds particular meaning for confronting contemporary expressions of human suffering and fragmentation in local and global spaces. Whenever the church creatively speaks and acts on behalf of and in solidarity with the powerless and marginalized groups, we concur with scholars across disciplines that it is in these moments when the church participates in God's work of reconciliation in the world. Structural and systematic issues such as poverty, healthcare, incarceration, and escalating militarism must begin to take center stage in theological discourse and the church's mission in the world.

The idea of reclaiming prophetic dimensions of the Christian heritage arises from the fact that God calls us to think and act in relation to all spheres of human experience—social, political, economic, and religious. What does it mean to be Christian in a context of social systems and structures that devalue and demean human life? Our point of departure is a belief that because God is the God of all creation, there are no realms outside of or beyond God's redemptive love and justice. God's love is not passive but active and transformative. Through the reconciling work of God in Christ, Christians are called to be agents of reconciliation and social transformation, called to participate in what God is doing in the world. We suggest that King's legacy of a beloved community offers a constructive theological and ethical perspective from which we can develop an inclusive vision of justice and reconciliation within the United States' religious context.

# Acknowledgments

We would like to thank our editor, Burke Gerstenschlager and his assistants Kaylan Connally, Lani Oshima, and Caroline Kracunas for their support from the inception of this project through its many iterations. We also want to thank Danielle Quinn for her assistance in verifying citations. We offer a special word of gratitude to Z Hall for her constructive responses.

# Not God Bless America, God Damn America: Black Rhetorical Performance and Patriotic Idealism

In April 2008, Angela D. Sims, then an instructor of Christian Ethics and Black Church Studies at Saint Paul School of Theology in Kansas City, Missouri, received a handwritten note from one of the seminary's donors asking Sims to elaborate on her comments in Helen T. Gray's Kansas City Star article "A Prophet in His Own Land."[1] In particular, the self-described "Methodist layman" wanted to know whether Sims' "apologist role is for the style of Wright's preaching only and not for the sulfuric anti-American content." Of particular concern for the writer was Sims' "analysis of Wright's statement [that]: The U. S. created the aids virus to infect Black Americans." He wanted to understand by "what standard could this outrageous statement be considered speaking truth to power as in prophetic preaching."

In her July reply, Sims stated that her comments were not an apology or defense of the Reverend Dr. Jeremiah A. Wright Jr.'s April 13, 2003, sermon "Confusing God and Government." Sims explained that Wright did not, as the sound bites might lead some to conclude, "damn America." What he did say, however, was

The government gives them the drugs, builds bigger prisons, passes a three-strike law, and then wants us to sing "God Bless

America." No, no, no. Not "God Bless America;" God Damn America! That's in the Bible, for killing innocent people. God Damn America for treating her citizens as less than human. God Damn America as long as she keeps trying to act like she is God and she is supreme!...Turn back and say "Forgive him for the 'God Damn,' that's in the Bible Lord." Blessings and cursing is in the Bible, it's in the Bible. But I'm fitting to help you one last time. Let me tell you something. Where governments fail, God never fails. (Jeremiah Wright, "Confusing God and Government," 2003)

At issue it appears, is who determines whether a country's actions are classified as homeland security or terrorism.

In her reply, Sims posited that though the writer defined the rhetoric of Wright as "angry vitriol [that is]...reprehensible and totally objectionable," perhaps we should, in a post 9/11 society, question the tendency to categorize counter perspectives as unpatriotic. After all, Wright is not the only preacher to voice concerns about governmental actions. Consider, for example, the following statements made by Reverends Jerry Falwell and Pat Robertson.

And I agree totally with you that the Lord has protected us so wonderfully these 225 years. And since 1812, this is the first time that we've been attacked on our soil and by far the worst results. And I fear, as Donald Rumsfeld, the Secretary of Defense, said yesterday, that this is only the beginning. And with biological warfare available to these monsters—the Husseins, the Bin Ladens, the Arafats—what we saw on Tuesday, as terrible as it is, could be miniscule, if, in fact—if, in fact—God continues to lift the curtain and allow the enemies of America to give us probably what we deserve. (Jerry Falwell, September 13, 2001 telecast of the *700 Club*)

Don't ask why did it happen. It happened because people are evil. It also happened because God is lifting His protection from this nation and we must pray and ask Him for revival so that once again we will be His people, the planting of His righteousness, so that He will come to our defense and protect us as a nation. That is what I want to see and why we say we must have revival. (Pat Robertson, Press Release regarding terrorist attack on the United States of America)

Even a cursory read of Falwell and Robertson's assessment of that fateful event in 2001 suggests that the media should have subjected their remarks to the same level of media scrutiny as that given to Wright's. Since there is no monolithic representation of life in the United States of America, Sims questioned whether the tone of delivery was equally important as the substance of Wright's message when one attempts to decide what is and what is not an acceptable representation of patriotism.

## Shaping Public Opinion

Pride in one's nation, a zealous devotion to its welfare, and a fervent loyalty to its government are the traditional markers of patriotism.[2] The handling of Wright, whose name was not nationally recognized by his critics before the 2008 presidential campaign, illustrates a manner in which reporters and broadcasters can and do shape public opinion. Broadcasters did not play Wright's recorded sermon in its entirety, thereby making it almost impossible for listeners to draw their own conclusions. Instead, character depictions accompanied most replays of the excerpts along with several reporters, anchors, and other public figures who described Wright's sermons as "animated," "ranting," "eardrum-assaulting," "offending," "divisive," "destructive," "racially charged," "black chauvinist rhetoric." They characterized his theological positions as "bad," "radical," "extreme separatist views," "stuck in a late-Sixties time warp," that "denigrate both the greatness and the goodness of our nation."[3]

These pejorative adjectives are clear examples of how language functions to elicit a desired response. An interdisciplinary approach to the study of "text in context" known as discourse analysis sheds light on how language functions in context through a critical evaluation of the properties of language. Utilizing this method often contributes to understanding some of the ways in which modes of communication can maintain privilege at the expense of denigrating others.[4]

More than five years after the 2008 airing of excerpts from Wright's sermon, an unquestioned depiction of Wright and a near-deafening silence on similar comments offered by Falwell, Robertson, and other self-identified evangelical pastors emphasizes that there is a mingling of the secular and the sacred in the sentiments of patriotism.[5] Yet, as Edward S. Herman and David Peterson posit, this episode provides an outstanding illustration of this country's racism, chauvinism, and political biases[6]. With virtually 24-hour news coverage, sound bites, and character depictions function subliminally, according to Alan Geyer, as patriotic rhetoric to sanctify racism, sexism, antiunionism, excess profits, witch hunts, religious bigotry, and environmental plunder.[7] At issue for us, though, is not an examination of this country's cloaked racist ideology but rather what presented during the 2008 presidential campaign as nonawareness, not of black prophetic preaching, but, of the tradition of the American jeremiad in which Wright's sermon, "Confusing God and Government," must be understood.

## American Rhetorical Theory and Practice

In the history of this republic, enslaved persons of African descent, classified as chattel for economic- and 3/5 human for political- purposes, were the only people legally forbidden to learn to read and write. From their arrival in what is now the United States, Africans and their descendants were viewed as pagan. Yet, as sociologist W. E. B. Du Bois documented in *The Negro Church*,[8] the first full-length treatment of the Black Church in the United States, in the seventeenth century there was a positive refusal to let slaves be converted, and this refusal was one incentive to explicit statements of the doctrine of perpetual slavery for Negroes.[9] Evidence does suggest, however, that there was some effort to convert slaves as early as 1624, blacks' baptisms were recorded in church registers.[10] Though the bible was used by many slave holders and their sympathizers as a tool of subjugation and control, historians provide numerous accounts of enslaved, freed, and free persons of color's ability to engage in a process of scriptural interpretation that reflected their existential reality. From this emerged a faith that bore witness not to a God that condoned slavery but rather a testimony about a God who "set captives free." From this biblically informed understanding of liberation emerged the "Invisible Institution."[11] In designated spaces that allowed for freedom of expression, blacks exercised moral agency.

Cognizant of risks associated with unauthorized public gatherings, enslaved persons gathered in "hush harbors," and other locales where they were not subjected to oversight by slave owners or their representatives. With what Walter Brueggemann might describe as "faithful imagination"[12] the ability to read printed words was not a prerequisite to either a personal relationship with God or a call to preach. Some scholars draw correlations between this emphasis on personal conversion, coupled with freedom of expression in worship, to revival movements dating back to the early 18th century, from which blacks drew on and adapted their cultural memories[13] to negotiate public and private spaces. Of utmost significance is the importance of the preached word as a major aspect of the United States' jeremiad, albeit with particular reference to what is now the United States. To this end, we posit that what we learn about views on preaching, theology, rhetorical styles, social customs, and understanding of preacher as pastor-citizen from preachers from varied historical epochs and perspectives is essential to understanding the ways in which media interpretations of rhetorical performance influences idealistic perceptions of patriotism.

### Clergy's Most Important Duty

Described as a leading figure of the Great Awakening in the Middle Colonies, Gilbert Tennent[14] was, according to some, one who questioned the traditional authoritarian system and the hierarchical structure of society and asserted that social position does not determine a person's true character. Born in Ireland in 1703, Tennent was 14 years old when his family came to America. With an MA from Yale, Tennent, as Janet

F. Fishburn points out, "distinguished himself from his peers in his ability to adapt old world theology, ministry practices, and policy selectively to a very different set of circumstances in a new world."[15] It is this ability to contextualize ministry that informed both Martin Luther King Jr.'s and Jeremiah Wright's sermonic structure and delivery.

Intimately acquainted with race, particularly a sociocultural construction of a black/white dichotomy in the United States, both preachers' engagement with the biblical text was informed by a historical analysis with which their faith resonated. Refusing to ignore the crucible of Jim Crow that symbolized neo-slavery and to romanticize West Africa as a place of genealogical-spiritual connectivity, King and Wright developed an amazing ability to theologically interpret political decisions. Yet, for many, King's public delivery of his dream is all too often presented as a parody to counter Wright's public proclamation of national accountability. In its depiction of Wright as an anathema to King, a shift from focusing on preaching as performance to a substantive assessment of the sermon itself can function as a framework to mediate conversations on race, rather than a media demand that a presidential candidate denounce pastor and church publicly, in the United States of America.

Convinced that the sermon was the clergy's most important duty, Dennis Barone identifies two essential tasks that characterize Tennent's preaching—(1) the communication of what he called a "historical faith," that is, the laity's understanding of and assent to Christianity's essential doctrines and (2) aiding the Holy Spirit in providing an "experimental Knowledge" of that divine grace that transformed the mental historical faith of the believer into the heartfelt experiential faith found only in converted Christians.[16]

Tennent knew the power of words and believed rhetors could use this power for good or ill. On the one hand, he viewed persuasion, especially that which incited action, as beneficial. On the other hand, he considered language that sought merely to please detrimental.[17] His concept of an ideal preaching ministry reflects a methodology that is described as the "preaching of the terrors." Or as Julius H. Rubin notes, Tennent's homiletical approach "stuck down the unconverted and coldhearted alike, awakening them to the perils of their condition. Those who came under his masterful rhetoric felt that he spoke directly, intimately, to the personal state of their souls."[18] For Tennent, the harsh reality of sin's consequences had to alarm the sinner before the soothing balm of gospel promises could properly be applied to calm the convicted and to strengthen the converted. The preaching of the terrors, which Tennent declared was the proper method of a saving ministry, was the first of a two-step homiletic process by which a minister led his congregation to conversion.[19]

Throughout most of his career, Tennent used the traditional Puritan sermon form and emphasized emotion over intellect.[20] From his earliest sermons to his last, he embedded all appeals to his audiences, whether to their hearts or to their minds, in the sermon in the form of text, doctrine, reason, and application.[21] Among the rhetorical devices Tennent frequently used were subdivisions, direct address, repetition, extensive Biblical quotations, similes, illustrative metaphors, occasional poetic couplets, alliteration, rhetorical question, and imagery.[22] He argued that appeals to both the intellect and the passions were necessary for the most effectual preaching.[23] He cautiously added that excessive emotional appeal led to over-zealous enthusiasm.[24]

With an adaptive and conciliatory demeanor,[25] Tennent "came to emphasize a religion of the head as well as one of the heart,"[26] a lifestyle of stability and cultural influence as well as one of emotions and strenuous reform. His works reveal a more practical man whose primary concern was the adjustment of his thought and rhetoric for the most effective promotion of conversion and the practice of piety.[27]

Tennent's contributions to American preaching are a poignant reminder that the contextual nature of history requires an awareness of the pluralistic nature of contemporary interpretations and subsequent applications. His influence on preaching in the United States is still relevant. In particular, we note the following observations. First, Tennent's maturation as a preacher points to the complexity of sermon preparation that demands an intentional attentiveness to the concerns and needs of the listening audience. And, Tennent's homiletical style may be used as a method against which to compare and contrast characteristics associated with African American preaching in a way that invites informed critical thinking and analysis.

## A Radical Shift in Evangelistic Methods

Charles Grandison Finney[28]—teacher, lawyer, pastor, theologian, and college president—is recognized as the father of revivalism in the United States. Though Dwight Lyman Moody[29]—entrepreneur, lay evangelist, and "self-made" man— is perhaps the most widely known and respected revivalist in the United States during the last third of the nineteenth century. Finney and Moody are, in many respects, both a study in contrast and similarity for anyone interested in identifying the source of contemporary Protestant practices and analyzing its practices in the United States.

Finney, perhaps best described as both a visionary and a man of his time, believed that the clerical traditions of the seventeenth and eighteenth centuries were aristocratic and obsolete. As such, he suggested that existing ministerial customs must give way to a new and liberal outlook if the nation was to enjoy peace, liberty, and prosperity under God. Finney's pietistic evangelicalism, however, made him see politics through moralistic eyes and he cast his vote in terms of particular moral issues rather than in terms of party politics.[30]

We posit that King and Wright's faith in a God who sets captives free empowered them to name the United States' sin of racism and militarism in unambiguous terms. Perhaps it is the power of their messages, replete with indictments supported by documented evidence, which inevitably led to the Federal Bureau of Investigation's heightened scrutiny of King's activity and the media's castigation of Wright and a theology of liberation that emerges from and is informed by black's lived reality in this republic. Yet, we realize that a detailed analysis of Wright's vocabulary contrasted against that of Falwell and Robertson's responses to the 9/11 attacks will more than likely yield immensely different media reactions. It is quite plausible that the very persons who lauded Falwell and Robertson's claims that the terror of that horrendous day was God's response to national sin may be the same individuals who denounced Wright for his critique of what we characterize as civil religion that makes no distinction between God and the United States. Perhaps a theological truth that many may have grasped had they listened to Wright's sermon, "Confusing God and Government", is that idolatry in any form that seeks to justify unethical behavior should evoke a counter response from the church.

Yet, Finney's ability to employ both reason and understanding to assess the affect of culture on religion and politics contributed to what many describe as a radical shift in evangelistic methods.[31] Among the practices that he introduced, which several Protestant denominations still employ, are the (1) participation of women in corporate worship, (2) use of colloquial language in sermons and prayers, (3) reliance upon novelty and excitement, (4) home visitations, (5) persuasive rhetoric, (6) ability to reach and touch every class of people, and (7) passionate espousal of moral reforms.[32]

Although never ordained, Moody learned from industrialists how to make revivalism a big business by transforming Finney's revival techniques.[33] Though he did not possess charisma as a preacher, Moody possessed the special power to touch the common people and brought a businessman's common sense to revival work while at the same time perpetuating a status quo position on racial segregation. While some posit he believed in the constant presence and guidance of the Holy Spirit and concentrated his efforts to "urbanize" revivalism as part of a general struggle to adapt a traditional faith to a rapidly changing external environment others question Moody's motives and practices.[34]

Moody's insight led him to understand the significance of training new converts to become active in evangelistic initiatives.[35] Hence, his ingenuity to identify and implement alternative modes of ministry outreach and corporate worship continue to shape the direction of "trends" in contemporary Protestantism in the United States. Some current religious practices attributed to Moody are (1) solicitation techniques to generate interest in "preaching meetings," (2) concept of evangelistic teams, (3) home-based prayer meeting, (4) informal speaking techniques, (5) incorporation of stories, (6) stressing of a simple message of a God of love rather than a God of wrath and judgment, and (7) creation of church-sponsored schools for lay evangelists.[36]

Using the power of prayer and publicity, Moody staged citywide crusades that became civic spectacles.[37] And while he is often credited with forging the bond between revivalism and mass media, Moody and Finney were both great advertisers. Although Finney believed that individuals are saved only by the grace of God, he, like Moody, used multiple advertising means.[38]

Today, an investigation of the use of mass media to "promote" religion can function as a framework to analyze Finney's and Moody's influence on contemporary US Protestantism. For instance, television networks owned and controlled by religious organizations may lead to an erosion of civil liberties as they capitalize on their business and political connections as well as a vehicle by which to manipulate public opinion. In addition, as memberships in the most popular denominations reach and exceed five thousand, the implementation of home-based prayer meetings—"marketed" as small groups, cell groups, or other trendy labels—may foster a dependence on predetermined responses in order to promote a façade of unity that is deliberately structured to avoid addressing issues that may challenge the validity of the ministry. Also, the self-promotion of "celebrity" revivalists may contribute to the amassing of debt by individuals who become mesmerized by the "hype" created by individuals who misappropriate the gospel. Given these concerns, Finney and Moody provide a historical framework for an ethical, sociological, and/or anthropological analysis of contemporary popular religion, when placed in dialogue with King and Wright, from which to engage in a deconstructive examination of varied meanings US citizens ascribe consciously or not to "in God we trust" and "God bless America."

## Skillful Blending of Politics and Religion

Widely acknowledged as the most eloquent preacher of his day, Henry Ward Beecher[39] was a born fighter for what he deemed truth and liberty. This is perhaps illustrated in his skillful blending of politics and religion. A fearless and powerful speaker, Beecher, like Martin Luther King Jr., was a leader of leaders who touched human life at almost every point. Described as a magnificent force in moral reform and a great editor and author, Beecher was instrumental in influencing political action.[40]

Beecher's preaching had a quality so distinct and original that it cannot be easily classed with that of any other master of pulpit eloquence. As a preacher for and to the people, Beecher regarded preaching as the highest of all earthly pursuits. Preeminent for his preaching of "heart religion" based on the "personality of Christ," Beecher's theory of preaching emerged from and was informed by his personal experience of God's grace and his understanding of vocation. While not formulaic in a prescriptive sense, Beecher's theory of preaching comprised four elements that are perhaps best described as relational oriented. According to him, effective proclamation is evidenced by one's willingness and ability to (1) preach the Gospel of Jesus Christ; (2) have Christ so melted and dissolved in you that when you preach you preach Christ as Paul did; (3) have every part of you living and luminous with Christ, and then to make use of everything that is in you; and (4) take everything that is in you all steeped in Jesus Christ, and throw yourself with all your power upon a congregation.[41]

Beecher had all the requisites of a great preacher, and all of them in superabundant force and fullness. He loved God and people and had a prophet's power and a prophet's susceptibility. Regardless of the sermon's subject, during the last 30 years of his preaching four great thoughts are reflected in every sermon: (1) his conception of the suffering God; (2) his conception of the divinity of Jesus Christ, (3) the sanctity of the individual, and (4) the certainty of the soul's immortality. However loft his idealism and "eagle-winged his flights of imagination," there was always a healthy and strong foundation of sturdy common sense that may be truly called a general characteristic of his preaching.[42]

Always a preacher, Beecher was a man of action. Religion, according to him, was the cohesive force that prevented the fragmentation and disintegration of the social order. It is worth noting that some suggest that Beecher was a political reformer only because he believed that the gospel was social as well as individual. Yet as an adviser to presidents and chaplain to an entire nation, he had a hand in shaping the United States' emergent civil religion.[43]

Recognized by many as the chief champion in the New World of the pulpit's duty to apply Christianity to all the great ethical concerns of business and society, Beecher was extremely sensitive to what he deemed injustice. Because the controversies of his time involved all the principles of humanity and of religion, he was drawn into political controversy and agitation. As a result, he gained a worldwide reputation as a political and social reformer. His activity with voice and pen was constant and intense and included critical analysis of both sides of a national dilemma. He had the courage of his convictions in religion, economics, and politics—and he made other men as brave as himself. Hence, he devoted his career to meeting the crisis of faith by setting forth in his sermons and lectures a new middle-class ethos built around a more personal and intuitive belief in Christianity.[44]

Considered a pioneer among preachers who have learned to bring truth down to date, Beecher moved on people through the conscience before appealing to emotion and sentiment. In many ways, the wholesomeness of his preaching is its close practical connection with all human life. In his ethical passion he made religion one with righteousness, in his patriotic passion he made it one with country and humanized religion for the United States of America. In light of what may be tentatively defined as an emergence, or perhaps reemergence, of US civil religion in a post 9/11 society, a critical comparative assessment of Beecher's practices can both clarify and provide a framework against which to evaluate contemporary applications of his practices. Echoes of Beecher reverberate in many preaching platforms, to include that of Jeremiah Wright, and yet, the ability to critique multiple perspectives of a burgeoning national dilemma appears to be a distinctively missing, but necessary, element.

### Shared Histories from a Different Worldview

Historian of Religion Charles H. Long is correct to remind us that the context of the black prophetic tradition must be seen as a protest against a hegemonic, enslaving, and oppressive situation. He is also forthright in his assertion that the black prophetic tradition in the United States is a unique and specific meaning of the nature of religious prophesy and that it has much to contribute not only to the meaning of prophesy itself but also to political thought and the necessary but subtle relationship between religion and politics in the modern world.[45] It is a world, so aptly demonstrated by many political pundits during the 2008 and reinforced during the 2012 presidential campaigns, that wants to proclaim the advent of a postracial society devoid of any serious critique or analysis of race as a product of social-cultural imagination. It is, perhaps, this worldview, that Wright's sermon, "Confusing God and Government" disrupted.

As Traci C. West aptly notes, racial logics based on denial abound in our society.[46] West's claim emerges from and is informed by her research on the intersectionality of race, gender, and sexual violence. If, however, history is a keeping of records, we contend that mythological representations of the United States as a moral exemplar in a global society can, as illustrated by reactions to Wright's sermon, "have a profound impact upon one's ability to integrate universal moral concerns with particular ones."[47]

Given an almost unquestioned assumption that the United States is a Christian nation, Wright's hypothesis that even when governments lie, fail, and change, God never fails may be viewed as an indictment against an implied universal construction of culture that devalues pluralistic perspectives. With great regard for contributions and sacrifices made on behalf of this country by active duty and reserve military personnel and their families, Wright's incessant sound bite, "God damn America," disrupted a political narrative that equates religion and patriotism as irrevocably synonymous. Or, as Martin Luther King Jr.[48] opined in his April 30, 1967, sermon "Why I Am Opposed to the War in Vietnam," there are those who seek to equate dissent with disloyalty.[49]

Acclaimed worldwide for his nonviolent response to American apartheid practices, King's social-ethical critique of our country's "triple evils of racism, economic exploitation, and militarism"[50] was not an unpatriotic, rhetorical proclamation. Rather, it was out of an immense sense of moral responsibility informed by a deep commitment to the gospel and love of country that King opposed the Vietnam War. Without reverting to phraseology, such as that employed by Wright and subsequently acknowledged minutes later as inappropriate, King shifted from an integrationist approach that was at least tolerable on many accounts to one that outlined contradictions in democratic claims that many interpreted as unpatriotic. Almost one year before he was assassinated, King's rhetorical performance at Riverside Church in New York City, without any change to his customary delivery or style, resonates with a tradition that is endemic of both the American jeremiad and a black preaching tradition.

## Embodied African American Preaching Tradition

A fourth generation preacher, Martin Luther King Jr. discovered his identity and calling in the church. King, an African Baptist, was the product of a preaching tradition that valued originality of effect above originality of composition.[51] Based on this understanding of preaching, it is suggested, as Richard Lischer explains, that King recognized that "a sermon is meant to be a vehicle of something greater than itself."[52]

In a manner reflective of his inherited tradition, when it came to preaching, King "relied on what had been given to him."[53] He learned to preach primarily through emulation of accomplished preachers and his fitness to preach was affirmed through demonstration.[54] King's preaching was an electrifying moment, but only a moment, in which he merged his voice with the tradition's continual cry.[55] Thus, every sermon outline King received he necessarily adapted to his own context and used in service of the one and only intellectual passion of his life, the argument for freedom.[56]

While King may not have read the bible as an "inexhaustible encyclopedia of life,"[57] he did, however, routinely cite the Bible as the authority for his social activities, and cast the civil rights movement in the light of biblical events and characters.[58] He sprinkled his sermons with brief, concise, and balanced maxims reminiscent of the Book of Proverbs and other Hebrew poetry.[59] Ultimately, King let the church guide his interpretation.[60] At Ebenezer Baptist Church in Atlanta, Georgia, he preached explicitly from bible texts[61] and the specificity of race sharpened the point of his biblical interpretation and preaching.[62]

What moved his audiences were the formulas and set pieces he skillfully inserted into his sermons and speeches.[63] King's sermons were imaginative, narrative, and likely to generate an experiential encounter. Repetition was an essential ingredient in what is referred to as the King sound.[64] This perhaps contributed to his ability to establish a near-hypnotic rhythm by which he induced pleasure in his audience, won its assent, and ideally, energized it for action in the community or nation.[65]

By learning how to follow the emotional curve of a religious idea as it took possession of a congregation,[66] King demonstrated an ability to respond to the movement of the Spirit between preacher and people and to express deep feeling without shame. He drew rhetorical energy from lively audiences and in turn energized them in a unique way. The response to King's preaching signified the communal nature of preaching and biblical interpretation in the black church. This act of participatory proclamation to help King "make it plain" resulted in the completion of his sentences, especially his recitations of scripture, by echoing his words, and by responding with encouragement and joy.[67] Eventually, King came to understand call and response as but a dress rehearsal for the community's social performance of the Word of God.[68]

King was, as Lischer asserts, in the fullest and most positive sense of the word, an actor.[69] Viewing the sermon as an "oral performance of Scripture"[70] that includes the whole congregation, he had the preacher's knack of translating every stray piece of information into the dramatic communication of ideas. It has been suggested that King's ability to dramatize ideas made him the most formidable orator in the United States.[71] In addition, his ability to treat the congregation as the conscience or guardian of the community frequently resulted in his audiences responding by playing the chorus to his lead.[72]

A descendant of those who gathered in hush harbors that comprised the "invisible institution," King's religious heritage trained him to see realities to which others were blind. From the beginning of his career King embraced his prophetic role, attaching it both to his work for racial equality and his broader advocacy of peace and economic justice.[73] With a prophet's eye for seeing local injustices in the light of transcendent truths, King was forced to confront the evil all around him and fight it to the death. In his prophetic ministry, King gave names to what he saw: sin, racism, genocide, doom, cowardice, expediency, and idolatry of nation, militarism, and religious hypocrisy.[74] He raised the eyes of his congregation by means of a rich assortment of poetic techniques. But before he exercised his gift of speaking, he practiced the poet's—and the prophet's—gift of seeing while employing his oratory to build a public consensus.[75]

Drawing on his training in the black preaching tradition, King was ever the prepared and public man.[76] Recognized as the first theological thinker since the Social Gospel movement to forge a synthesis of evangelical and liberal traditions in America,[77] shuttling between innumerable audiences, he was proficient in crafting his messages to the capacities of his varied audiences.[78] And yet, his ability to communicate with more than one audience did not compromise his moral vision or quiet his prophetic rage. King dared to dream a world where justice and righteousness would flow freely and exercised the moral courage to critique a nation and call it to account for its injustices. The sound of the drumbeat that galvanized him to action, though muffled, continues to echo not only in the black church but also in the world. Living as we do in a world where war is often a preferred recourse to achieve a desired outcome, King invites us, and others who share in and stand in solidarity with this African American preaching tradition, to seek creative and constructive ways to embody the richness of an inherited legacy that is so much more than a "theatrical whoop."

## A Concluding Thought

As religious scholars in nonhistorical and rhetorical disciplines, we acknowledge that a better understanding of the United States' jeremiad warrants extensive study, particularly in an era where we can disseminate sound bites around the globe in nano seconds. Informed by historical and contextual realities, rhetorical theory and practice is also embodied performance that employs language symbolically to engage a listening audience. With a growing dependency on media to shape public opinion, it is incumbent that we address how discourse is deployed skillfully to foster a form of intellectual and spiritual genocide. Stated another way, a review of both media and black community responses to King's "Why I Am Opposed to the War in Vietnam" and Wright's "Confusing God and Government" may suggest a need to examine carefully the manner in which the study of text in context is employed to divert attention from underlying issues that often contributes to our inability to recognize and subsequently minimize effects associated with unquestioned acceptance of patriotic ideology. Failure to engage in this constructive assessment exacerbates a culture of xenophobia.

# 2

## Disturbing the Peace: Theological Mandate to Construct an Inclusive Vision of Humanity

In light of visual depictions of Obama as nonhuman[1] it is hard to imagine seven words, "life, liberty, and the pursuit of happiness," having more meaning than what they supposedly represent to a population segment that has garnered much media attention in the current political climate in the United States.[2] These concluding words in the first sentence of the second paragraph of "The unanimous Declaration of the thirteen united States of America" have, since 1776, shaped a civil and theological narrative defined by slavery, reconstruction, Jim Crow, and Civil Rights initiatives. These epochs determined, to a great extent, how particular population segments interpreted and applied concepts that are foundational to what it means to be an "American." A primary premise, irrespective of ethnicity, is a concept of inherent "rights" for all people. Given a yet emerging national conversation about constitutional interpretation and application, we question whether contemporary meanings of "life, liberty, and the pursuit of happiness" are informed by a literal approach that fails to address historical complexities. At the same time, we seek to determine whether we can reclaim or perhaps offer a more nuanced analysis of these key terms, which continue to inform national identity and notions of patriotism, in order to articulate a doctrine of humanity that will encourage us to examine polarities attributed to our individual and collective understanding of these words.

In recent times, individuals often focus on the loss of life, liberty, and the pursuit of happiness as the interpretive lens for these words.[3] This emphasis, most recently associated with persons affiliated with the Tea Party, has garnered significant media attention. For example, in a 2010 timesunion.com blog, the author Valerie Doane noted that, "There's a growing fear among many Americans that we are losing our rights and freedoms. I share that fear although honestly, our rights and freedoms have slowly and methodically been chipped away long before the current administration came into power. The only difference is that now the "chipping away" is accelerated and therefore more noticeable to everyday Americans."[4] She is vague in defining what liberties we have lost, but infers somehow our inalienable rights are gradually deteriorating.

The historical basis of the Tea Party movement comes from the Boston Tea Party of 1773 and the protest of higher taxes on tea.[5] The original Boston Tea Party was about disturbing the peace and making it known to the monarchy that the colonies believed their rights were being abused. Samuel Adams was one of the lead figures in the Boston Tea Party event of throwing the tea into the water.

The actions of Adams and others involved in the original Boston Tea Party movement are perceived as laying the groundwork for the way we should interpret "life, liberty, and the pursuit of happiness." These words imbue individuals with certain freedoms that cannot be taken away or denied. Individuals have a right to protest or to disturb the peace when their inalienable rights are being denied. The new Tea Party movement believes it is functioning out of this same understanding of inalienable rights. Therefore the depictions of Obama as nonhuman by some in the movement should not be interpreted as racist, but an effort to protect the inalienable rights of citizens. The questions is: "Whose rights are being protected?"

The words life, liberty, and pursuit of happiness were not included in the initial draft of the Declaration of Independence. In his 1772 treatise, "The Rights of the Colonists," Samuel Adams used similar language.[6] According to Adams, the natural rights of humans are life, liberty, and property.[7] Adams sticks with the language of property, which has important historical ramifications for those who did not own property or were categorized as property by law. Attention must be given to the motive for these claims if we are to understand their significance in a twenty-first century global society in which the United States continues to promote itself as a world leader.

Totally oblivious to the historical era in which Adams lived, some suggest he perceived the law of God as superseding all other laws in terms of natural rights. If this position is accepted without question, how then do we account for the many, whether slaves, white women, or unpropertied white men, who by virtue of social categorization, gender, or class were denied rights granted to land-owning white men? By excluding targeted populations from the working definition, did Adams and others, who appropriated John Locke's concept of natural rights, create sub-classes of humanity and in so doing grant privilege to a select group of white men in order to solidify that they and they alone are endowed with certain rights?[8] Following this line of thinking, the role of government is to protect these rights.[9] Since the role of government is to in no way oppress the natural rights of humanity, how might an historically informed theological assessment of Adams' words further an understanding of "life, liberty, and the pursuit of happiness" that shapes how we "disturb the peace" in order to contribute to the common good?

In his 1772 report, Adams, in response to British imposed taxation system in the colonies, noted astutely that the "governors have no right to seek and take what they please." Adams makes a convincing case that the government has overstepped its boundaries and trampled the inalienable rights of the colonists. The British government's actions were conceived as an overreach of power that negated its institutional purpose to defend and protect.

Doane, a Tea Party member, asserts that anything the government does outside of defending the natural rights of citizens is overstepping the boundaries of government. Proponents of this movement insist, for instance, that taxes and health care are outside the government's spectrum. Advocates of this position, argue, at least in theory, in favor of restricted government power and intervention at the federal level. Of course, there are numerous examples of Tea Party members who are Medicare/Medicaid recipients as well as persons who question the government's inability to create jobs, which illustrates there are conflicting ideas of government and the ways in which its role as servant to the people is perceived.

How then, are we to interpret a rallying cry by Tea Party members and others who insist that Congress, and thus the United States of America, needs to govern in a manner that reflects the founding fathers' original intent? Of course, this almost inevitably contributes to a tendency by some to project an ahistorical national narrative that fails to discuss in any depth those not considered fully human by Adams (e.g., African Americans and women). Adams writes, "The absolute rights of Englishmen and all freemen, in or out of civil society, are principally personal security, personal liberty, and private property." This ideal of life, liberty, and property means African slaves not only had no rights, but also as property they could not be taken from their owners. Adams who believed it was his God given right to disturb the peace by dumping tea in the water is not extending this same right to African slaves to disturb the peace because they are property by law. The easy way out is to argue that slavery is no longer an issue and that all persons enjoy the same rights.

Therefore, many in the Tea Party perceive themselves as addressing a political issue and not a racial one.[10] This view of government focuses on the founding fathers understanding of life as the preservation of society.[11] Liberty means that the government cannot set arbitrary laws over people, but is the body that makes sure laws are justly carried out.[12] For example, the Tea Party interprets this to mean the health-care bill is an arbitrary law and that the government has overstep its boundaries. Finally, the government has no right to take property from individuals.[13]

For Adams, liberty, and we can infer life, are defined by God.[14] Likewise, we only discover our true humanity in relationship to God. And yet, debates about the government's constitutionally defined role in the polis demands that we employ a process by which we examine issues of rhetoric, interpretation, and appropriation if we are to avoid a simplistic and misinformed analysis of eighteenth-century concepts are essential, we believe, to a twenty-first-century understanding of natural rights.

Interestingly, what is not explored by Adams or the Tea Party is Adams' understanding of the common good. Adams writes, "The natural liberty of man, by entering into society, is abridged or restrained, so far only as is necessary for the great end of society, the best good of the whole."[15] Adams leaves an opening for individual rights to be subsumed under the greater good of the society. Certainly, this is our read of Adams, but it opens up the possibility for moving what it means to be human in a different direction than just individual rights. It empowers all segments of society to disturb the peace in a way that points to a greater good for all people.

It is probable that some members of the Tea Party base their understanding of the government's role, in part, on Adams' late eighteenth-century position. At the same time, there is no doubt that there is evidence to suggest that some Tea Party adherents are interested primarily in individual rights and ignore seeking the common good. For example, any action by the government that imposes upon people is interpreted as an arbitrary law. It is this individualistic understanding of humanity that distorts notions of the common good and calls forth questions about personal and corporate responsibility to others. At issue is whether we are able to give voice to our xenophobia. For ultimately, if we fail to come to terms with our fear of the Other, the stranger, the enemy who is also our neighbor, we become co-conspirators with Tea Party members who do not want to create a space where being in relationship demands that we not only think about the common good but also seek forgiveness when we fail to stand with the least of these.

After all, we should not, as theologian Dwight Hopkins points out, want to, as some in the Tea Party have, succumb to demonic individualism.[16] This demonic individualism moves us back to the language of the pursuit of happiness. A demonic individualistic understanding of the pursuit of happiness is not about figuring out both-and options for all parties, but instead focuses on one's self-interest.[17] In other words, we must avoid a tendency for satisfying what would make us happy individually at the expense of the common good. Many in the Tea Party focus on the pursuit of happiness, as an endowed right that predicates an either/or solution to issues like health care. Representative Morgan Griffith stated, "As Virginians we did not accept the chains of George III nor will we accept the chains of ObamaCare."[18]

Griffith's comments suggest "ObamaCare" is oppressive in the same way England oppressed the colonies. Hopkins point is this mentality negates the ways in which the new health-care bill seeks to make resources accessible to those going without coverage. A different understanding of what it means to pursue happiness and ultimately to be human is at stake. The pursuit of happiness should not be about a form of individualized apathy that translates into a national demonization of those who either question this behavior or who are victims of this quest for self-gratification by any means necessary. It is essential, we believe, to reframe how we understand the pursuit of happiness. It is also essential to reframe how we think about what it means to be human and the ways in which we disturb the peace moving us toward both-and options as we think about our individual and collective humanity.

## Fully Human: Frederick Douglass and the Issue of Slavery

A literalist reading of the exclusive language in the Declaration of Independence grants privilege to a class of white men. It is this distinct group, if one follows a literalist reading, who are endowed with an innate sense of life, liberty, and the pursuit of happiness. Implicit in early interpretations regarding unquestionable rights is a cultural understanding that excluded both male slaves and freed men of color. It is perhaps no coincidence that abolitionist Frederick Douglass, himself a former slave, wrestled with and addressed inconsistencies in social constructs that characterized American practices.

Despite a prevalent tendency to find fault with the United States, European visitors considered this nation an exemplar of liberalism because of its popular culture, emphasis on equality, and wide suffrage. Thus, it is important to note that Douglass' July 4, 1852, speech to the Rochester Ladies Anti-Slavery Society raised questions that challenged this concept of American liberalism. Douglass stressed to his listeners that the Fugitive Slave Law is "one of the greatest infringements of Christian Liberty.[19] He also admonished both laity and clergy to consider the hypocrisy associated with "thanking God for the enjoyment of civil and religious liberty" while simultaneously remaining "utterly silent," and thus complicit, "in respect to a law which robs religion of its chief significance and makes it utterly worthless to a world lying in wickedness."[20]

Douglass points to the discrepancies between claims delineated in the Declaration of Independence and prevalent practices, in this instance slavery, in the United States. In fact, Douglass asked attendees "if it be not somewhat singular that, if The Constitution were intended to be, by its framers and adopters, a slave-holding instrument, why neither slavery, slaveholding, nor slave can anywhere be found in it."[21] Far from acquiescing with public opinion, Douglass noted with clarity that for enslaved and freed persons of color this country's "birthday of your National Independence, and your political freedom" characterized by "the rich inheritance of justice, liberty, prosperity and independence" did not extend to him.[22] Douglass declared to his audience that

> standing with God and the crushed and bleeding slave on this occasion, I will, in the name of humanity which is outraged, in the name of liberty which is fettered, in the name of The Constitution and the Bible, which are disregarded and trampled

upon, dare to call in question and to denounce, with all the emphasis I can command, everything that serves to perpetuate slavery—the great sin and shame of America![23]

More than 150 years after Douglass offered his extensive social analysis and view of liberty. The Tea Party while not advocating for slavery is disturbing the peace in a manner that dehumanizes Obama.[24] Douglass writes about the original Boston Tea Party "You can bare your bosom to the storm of British artillery to throw off a three-penny tax on tea; and yet wring the last hard earned farthing from the grasp of the black laborers of your country."[25] Douglass points out the contradiction of those willing to disturb the peace to avoid further taxation, but not extending this same grace to African Americans. The issue for Douglass is not in disturbing the peace, which is open to all individuals. The issue is understanding the way in which we disturb the peace has to be consistent with the claims we are making about being human. Douglass' point should cause The Tea Party to reflect deeper on its treatment of Obama versus its claims for the loss of humanity.

Theologically, this means the pursuit of happiness cannot fall into an either/or option. Douglass is holding all of us accountable to the standards, which we claim for our Christian tradition. He points that which is dehumanizing cannot be of God.[26] Those in the Tea Party movement who dehumanize Obama while claiming to uphold the intent of the forefathers need to expand their interpretive lens of what it means to be human. Douglass pushes us to consider, "How do we pursue happiness without de-humanizing others?" For Douglass an inability to engage this question at the deepest level means "our humanity is a base pretense and our Christianity is a lie."[27] The Tea Party, is not entirely inaccurate in the importance it places upon, life, liberty, and the pursuit of happiness, but in light of Douglass' speech have not fully considered how this should point us toward a different vision of humanity. About ten years after he delivered his July 4, 1853, speech, Douglass raised a question that presented a glimpse of such a vision. He asked, "Can the white and colored people of this country be blended into a common nationality, and enjoy together, in the same country, under the same flag, the inestimable blessings of life, liberty and the pursuit of happiness, as neighborly citizens of a common country?"[28] To his self-generated query, Douglass replied affirmatively.[29] Despite past and ongoing oppression experienced by African Americans, he believed it was possible for all persons to live in harmony and offered several points to substantiate his view.[30]

Douglass, informed by various perspectives on reason, spirituality, and morality, insisted that the humanity of African Americans must be acknowledged.[31] Interestingly, the heart of his argument is rooted in Anglo (e.g., those of African descent are not rationale like those of European descent) attempts to disprove the humanity of African Americans. In addition, Douglass cites a congressional attempt to pass a law forbidding African Americans to be superior to Anglos.[32] There would be no need for such a law if Anglos did not already believe African Americans to be human. The only reason to pass the law is to deny African Americans' humanity.

Douglass also argued that The Constitution was not written only for Anglos. He highlighted the fact that, "The Constitution, in its language and in its spirit, welcomes the black man to all the rights which it was intended to guarantee to any class of the American people."[33] Douglass contended that the laws of the land already included all people and that the founding figures did this intentionally.[34] What is necessary is for the United States to take seriously the preamble to The Constitution.[35] By doing this it lives out not only what it claims in The Constitution but also the famous seven words in the Declaration of Independence.

Not only did Douglass provide evidence to support his claim that African Americans were fully human as well as included in provisions outlined in The Constitution, he tackled one of the more heinous claims against African Americans, that blacks belong to an inferior race.[36] Douglass noted that this argument was used by many to justify the inhumane treatment of African Americans.[37] This is not a novel concept. Douglass discussed how Anglos in the United States are not the first to use this argument. A study of nations quickly reveals that oppressors always find a warrant for such oppression.[38] For Douglass, a present-ing question was "What constitutes inferiority?"[39] Referring to Socrates, Bacon, and others as examples of superior humans, Douglass quickly asserted that few of any race meet this stan-dard.[40] We should not, he contended, judge based on those at the top, but rather upon the ability of all to grow.[41] Douglass does not provide insights into what it means to grow, but one can infer his point is that no one norm can be set for determin-ing superiority.

Douglass, believing a new vision of humanity was possible, encouraged his listeners to imagine that they were standing "at the portals of a new world, a new life and a new destiny."[42] Through a variety of means, it was possible to adopt a new vision for all Americans that must move beyond traditional rhetoric that privileged some at the dehumanization of others. Unequivocally, Douglass suggested, "There is reason to believe that we may permanently live under the same skies, brave the same climates, and enjoy liberty, equality and fraternity in a common country."[43] However, all of this hinges on our ability to live up to, and live out the true meaning of life, liberty, and the pursuit of happiness.

What Douglass demands of us is no small feat. His depiction of the common good points us toward a vision of humanity pregnant with possibility. Douglass realized the importance of the Declaration of Independence's famous seven words and used them in both his July 4 and his 1863 speech[44] to hold the United States accountable to its own narrative. While life, liberty, and the pursuit of happiness are not the entirety of the United States' narrative, they certainly influence how we understand our and other's humanity. It is to a deeper theological analysis of humanity we now turn.

## What It Means to Be Human

A basic premise in this chapter is that the words life, liberty, and the pursuit of happiness are one of the major threads in the fabric of the United States' narrative. These terms signal what it means to be human even when individuals reside at opposite ends, or somewhere along a continuum, of a political spectrum. An understanding of self, for a majority of persons in this country, begins with the way we interpret these famous seven words. Because of this almost unquestioned assumption, we find something much more profound at stake when we consider how these words illumine basic understandings of humanity. Given our brief discussion of Samuel Adams and Frederick Douglass' interpretation of "life, liberty and the pursuit of happiness," some preliminary attention to Dwight Hopkins' anthropology within black theology is warranted.

Hopkins explores three categories—selves and the self, culture, and race—to explain what it means to be human.[45] It is imperative that we understand "what it means to be a human being, singularly and in community."[46] Hopkins argues that we cannot talk about an individual self without reference to a communal self and vice versa.[47] He does, however, privilege the communal self.[48] What Hopkins suggests is that no one exists in isolation; to exist means dependency on someone for birth (we cannot give birth to ourselves).[49] Who we are as individuals is not shaped in a vacuum, but as part of a web of relationships.

To be a self is to recognize we are born into a particular legacy that we do not control. For example, individuals cannot predetermine their race, culture, or historical milieu.[50] Hopkins is clear that this does not eliminate individual agency and the ability to alter certain factors.[51] This recognition of human as self does signal that as individuals influenced by Western culture we need to rethink the *a priori* individualism that permeates US culture. To be human is to be a self, but never a self in isolation from others and this includes others coming before and after.

For Hopkins this means that the collective interest takes priority over "individual self-interest."[52] Of utmost importance is a commitment to seek the common good for the community. Hopkins realizes this is challenging for many in the United States and may require a "basic sharing" that runs counter to rampant individualism.[53] Inherent in the language of being fully human is a notion that all members of society deserve not only basics (food, shelter, and clothing) but also "peace, freedom, respect, dignity, security, and satisfaction."[54] Although Hopkins does not use this language, the aforementioned values represent what it means to have life.

If God is the source of life then the Divine seeks peace, liberty, and so forth, for the created order. Or as Hopkins states, "If theology... tells us something about the nature of God, then theological anthropology brings insight into God's intent for human kind... between theos [God] and anthropos [humanity]."[55] God's intent for humanity is for us not simply to be alive, but that we become fully human. For Hopkins, this means being able to participate in life completely without worrying about basic needs or the things that make living vital.

Many people will agree, at least in part, with Hopkins' analysis. A challenge, however, is how we secure liberty, respect, and so forth. The distinction Hopkins seeks between individualism and individuality is not one people make easily. Individuality is positive because it points to the fact that we are all unique beings.[56] Individualism is the "warped focus on self."[57] While some Tea Party adherents perceive their rhetoric as a vehicle to further God's intent for humanity rather than individualistic, Powe thinks Hopkins is correct to suggest that some of the Tea Party's rhetoric, based on his understanding of humanity, have more to do with individualism. For example, Marilyn R. of Rhode Island states, "that God is our healer. I don't believe in doctors or medicine. It would be against my religious beliefs to go to a doctor, so why do I need healthcare?"[58] Her perspective using Hopkins criteria is individualistic because religion centers on her wants exclusive from the broader community.

Hopkins' discussion is extremely insightful in that it helps us to understand it is virtually impossible to talk about an extracted singular self that is separated from community. To be human is to recognize that even a self that intentionally separates from community still exists at all times in a web of relationships. Theologically this means we are called to seek the good of the other and not focus totally on our own self-interest. At the same time, there is no doubt that a primary challenge is how to create a society where all parties purpose to live in a manner where everyone strives to contribute to the well-being of all.

Second, Hopkins helps us to better understand the role of culture as it relates to humanity.[59] An examination of Hopkins' full analysis of culture falls outside the scope of this chapter. Instead, we focus on the divine and human relationship, with specific attention to Hopkins' understanding of theological anthropology as a cultural process "in which an ultimate intermingles with the penultimate (that is, the God-human connection is profoundly situated in culture)."[60] As a result of, or perhaps in response to, this Divine encounter we begin to shape and live out our understanding of God in culture.

The fact that God comes in human form into a particular culture gives us a clue to the meaning of true humanity. This meaning is expressed, for Hopkins, in Luke 4:18–19 and Isaiah 61.1. In these two verses, the divine consciously enters into systemic structures to point toward a Godly vision of life, liberty, and the pursuit of happiness.[61] God is interested in either eradicating or transforming systemic structures, so that the disenfranchised can experience true life and liberty. It is not an abstract work by God, but one in which God enters the particularity of the human situation to invite others to participate actively in the unfolding of the eschaton. For Hopkins, God disturbs the peace and invites us to do the same.

Furthermore, to understand what it means to be human is to live in the tension between ultimate and penultimate. It is to constantly struggle with the significance of God becoming human with an expressed purpose to transform systemic ills. Hopkins, using six categories articulated by Jesse N. Mugambi, captures this ongoing struggle as it relates to culture and the divine.[62]

These categories—politics, aesthetics, kinship, recreation, religion, and ethics—shape culture in such a way that they deal with very issue of life and death.[63] It is not possible to understand what it means to be human within a culture and to transcend that understanding without some reference to these categories. These typologies are foundational for framing the way the ultimate and penultimate intermingle in culture. One cannot talk about one of these dimensions of culture as penultimate without reference to an ultimate vision of society.

A part of being human is defining these seven categories and living them out in very practical ways. For Christians, this is done with a realization that God (ultimate) has impinged upon or been revealed in culture.[64] This revealing means culture as a whole is being transformed into something new that includes individual selves. Hopkins again emphasizes the relational aspect of humanity. Culture is an intersection of the ultimate and penultimate, this intersection points toward a vision of humanity that is more inclusive of the least.[65]

Hopkins focuses on those at the bottom and the possibilities of life and liberation for these individuals. The transformation of society is a commitment to those at the bottom, so that they can experience true liberation and life.[66] Powe believes some Tea Party members would take issue with Hopkins in this case and argue (politically) that he is promoting socialism. That is, Hopkins advances a theory that requires a distribution of wealth as an act of justice that contributes to the well-being of all. This appropriation of resources is opposed by some Tea Party advocates on the grounds that such an application contradicts their interpretation of life, liberty, and the pursuit of happiness.

Hopkins emphasizes why it is important to understand culture to be more inclusive of those relegated to inferior positions in society. Theologically, Hopkins pushes us to recover a biblical model of humanity based on the Luke-Acts community. The goal of which is to live a different way based on the common good of the entire community. This ideal is what is critical in pointing us toward a different vision of culture. Powe is suggesting, it is this vision that would put Hopkins at odds with some in the tea party.

Finally, Hopkins examines the correlation of race and humanity, especially within the United States. Hopkins outlines sociological and biological reasons for race. He concludes that the existential reality of blacks in the United States is informed by both.[67] All humans are by nature born with certain God given attributes that identify them racially. Using an example of a light skinned African American in another context not being labeled black,[68] Hopkins explains that, racial identification is often context specific.[69] In other words, Hopkins illustrates the way that nature and nurture work within the United States. Nature or creation does dictate that we are born with certain attributes, but nurture or socialization provides a framework for how we understand those attributes. In Hopkins' opinion, it is not possible to speak of nature and nurture as separate categories, since they intersect and thus inform one another.

Hopkins argues that race, based on a syncretistic (both biological and sociological) understanding, is a social construct.[70] Not just any social construct, but one aimed at maintaining white superiority.[71] A tension exists between the way in which people are created and the way society predetermines who people are.[72] For people of color in the United States this means the ideal of what it means to be human is racial.[73] Even discussions on what it means to be fully human are by default racial conversations in the United States. Figuring out what it means to be made in the image of God (imago Dei) requires a deconstructive and reconstructive process for people of color because the category human is not neutral. It is a racial category that privileges whites and treats people of color as second-class citizens.[74]

One ramification associated with white privilege is a destructive spirituality that perpetuates racial beings in the United States. Hopkins writes, "This spirituality burst forth from materiality but transcends each individual white person and subsequent white generations."[75] In other words, white privilege is such a part of what it means to be human in the United States that it has become invisible to many. To describe humanity is, by default, to discuss a constructed white understanding of humanity.

Hopkins, reflective of the vision for humanity articulated by Frederick Douglass, is optimistic. As Hopkins explains, it is possible to be liberated from this construct of humanity.[76] After all, as he points out, a socially constructed concept can also be dismantled.[77] It is our contention that Hopkins presents evidence from which we can begin to imagine a new humanity that more closely resembles what it means to be fully human in the manner in Christ. This understanding of humanity is about the liberation of both blacks and whites from a racial under-standing of personhood toward one that more closely resembles the imago dei.

This racial understanding of humanity has continuously plagued some who associate with the Tea Party. Andy Ostroy's Huffington Post's article "The Tea Party Movement Isn't about Racism? Ostroy observes,

> Contrary to how the movement is portrayed as a non-partisan, multicultural, age/gender-diverse "big tent," most Tea Baggers are wealthy, white Republican males over 45, according to the poll. The poll chillingly illustrates what's really at the core of the move-ment: intense frustration, anger and resentment over the belief that a black president is giving taxpayer handouts to other blacks. In fact, 25% believe the Obama administration favors blacks over whites. As the Times reports, they believe that "too much has been made of the problems facing black people.[78]

Ostroy highlights what Hopkins describes theologically about the understanding of humanity in the United States. Anyone who is perceived as pro-African American stands against a true understanding of what it is to be American, to be human, and ultimately, stands against life, liberty, and the pursuit of hap-piness. Some in the Tea Party are blind to the way in which they substitute an ideal of humanity for a construct of white humanity.

This lack of awareness is a major chasm that prevents a con-structive national conversation on race in the USA. Tea Party proponents can argue that anyone who suggests their movement is about racism does not understand that the movement's major impetus is political. This is where Hopkins insights are invalu-able. He points out that a person of color must, as a prerequisite for Tea Party acceptance, agree with a Tea Party understanding of humanity. What they call a neutral ideal of humanity (more likely what it means to be American) is really a privileging of white over black.

To recap, Hopkins gives us insight into the way that self/ selves, culture, and race intersect to shape multiple understand-ings of humanity. Each category is important in its own right.

However, their points of intersection provide a more detailed picture of what it means to be human in the United States. Powe's selection of examples from the Tea Party illumines why, on the one hand, a chasm exists between some Anglos and African Americans and, on the other hand, why both Anglos and African Americans need to rethink their understanding of humanity. Disturbing the peace cannot simply be about individualtistic gain. Powe is suggesting disturbing the peace has to be about seeing and helping all in society to become more human. For Hopkins, this is the eschatological hope we have in God and it is to this eschatological hope that God calls us to participate.

## Human Flourishing

Life, liberty, and the pursuit of happiness in the United States have everything to do with what it means to be human. A major challenge is how to find a way for these seven words to be inclusive for all people rather than to benefit a few. Douglass' words, "there is reason to believe that we may permanently live under the same skies, brave the same climates, and enjoy liberty, equality and fraternity in a common country,"[79] resonate with us and invite us to engage in a serious dialogue about race relations in this country. In spite of, for example, the United States' legacy of racial and gender oppression, Douglass believed a new vision of humanity was possible. For Douglass this new vision was grounded, to a large degree, in the seven words "life, liberty, and the pursuit of happiness." We offer three suggestions that will enable us to live into Douglass' vision for humanity.

First, we must deepen our understanding of life. Life is not simply existence or surviving under the worst conditions. Life is a gift from God. Since all humans are created in God's image, we should be given an opportunity to flourish in our respective environments. To flourish goes beyond food, clothing, and shelter, to include safety and a concept of well-being. Called to practice this form of flourishing, we must engage in a constant socially informed individual assessment that informs a just redistribution of resources so that we seek consistently to ensure that individuals have what they need to live into their full potential.

To practice flourishing in this manner requires that we adopt a new vision of humanity. We have to truly see others as made in the image of God. As noted previously, a major challenge in the United States is white supremacy as a historically constructed ideology that privileges Anglos over African Americans. While there are many who refuse to acknowledge this reality and the diverse ways in which it manifests itself in this country, we must recognize that we have lost sight of true citizenry whereby the goal is to make sure everyone has access and can contribute in positive ways to society. Simply having a vote gives one an opportunity to participate in the creation of a "more perfect union." Yet, this expression of citizenship does not guarantee how we interact with others. How we contribute to society is contingent on our ability to rethink the importance of self in relation to our willingness to be more inclusive of selves. To live into this vision of humanity is to recognize that "I am because you are!"

Second, we must deepen our understanding of liberty. Liberty is not simply a right to satisfy individual desires. In fact, liberty should be perceived from the perspective of persons subjected to dehumanizing and demeaning practices. Human flourishing in this instance is an ability to exist without structures of oppression and to think creatively about ways in which we use our various points of privilege to benefit others. We must be careful, then, to distinguish liberty from our individual wants and to name accurately oppressive acts.

To practice flourishing is to recognize what is required in order to achieve a balance between what we want and to stand in solidarity with the oppressed. To accept this notion as a given is to acknowledge that everyone must sacrifice so that others can enjoy liberty. While individual rights are important, we can never forget that we all participate in the common good. This shared perspective does not mean we abandon individual rights. Instead, this relational understanding does require that we become more intentional to familiarize ourselves with our respective communities so that we become informed and active contributors to the common good.

Third, we must deepen our understanding of the pursuit of happiness. The pursuit of happiness does not endorse the accumulation of resources for selfish purposes. Human flourishing in this instance recognizes that because resources are limited we have a responsibility to ensure an equitable distribution system is implemented. This is not a call to some radical redistribution of resources. Rather, it is a call to rethink what is needed for happiness. But how do we measure happiness?

To practice flourishing means that we not only wrestle with how much is too much, but we also give serious consideration to deeper issues of happiness. In the United States, we have developed a perspective of happiness that promotes competition over others instead of collaboration with others. The ability to rethink the pursuit of happiness as a validation of everyone's humanity and not dehumanizing some for the benefit of others is more in line with Douglass' vision for humanity. The goal is not creating losers, but seeking a way we all can flourish together.

Intricately connected to a central United States of America narrative, "life, liberty, and the pursuit of happiness" convey our core beliefs about humanity. Unfortunately, an unwillingness on the part of one too many citizens to participate in the eradication of systems designed to thwart a specific peoples' well-being creates an idealized humanity from which only a few benefit. To reclaiming Douglass' vision of a new humanity that transforms these hope-filled words into a lived reality is a step in the right direction that requires us to deconstruct and reconstruct what it means to be human in the United States of America in this age of globalization that connects us to countless others. It requires us to disturb the peace in a way that all can flourish and does not privilege the wants of a few over everyone else.

# 3

## Liberation for All

We just argued that taking the words life, liberty, and the pursuit of happiness seriously can have significant implications for our collective humanity. It is interesting that President Obama began his second term with a focus on this phrase by distinguishing between concepts of "self-evident and self-executing."[1] Obama suggests that while life, liberty, and the pursuit of happiness are obvious rights, these rights are not always practiced. His inaugural speech emphasized a need to bridge the gap between what is obvious and a need to make the obvious habituated practices.

Obama clearly had in mind Martin Luther King Jr.'s "I Have a Dream" speech when he developed his inaugural speech. King's famous words from this particular speech suggested of the Declaration of Independence: "They were signing a promissory note to which every American was to fall heir."[2] According to King, this promissory note grants to all individuals, irrespective of ethnicity, a right to life, liberty, and the pursuit of happiness.[3] Like King, Obama's understanding of the promissory note is not racial but plays off of the ideal that every American, and even immigrants seeking to be US citizens, has a right to life, liberty, and the pursuit of happiness.

One of the challenges that we contend with currently is how to define the government's role in making sure life, liberty, and the pursuit of happiness are not merely words, but attainable ideals for all. Obama conjured up images of King as a way to set the agenda for his second term in which he sought to define the government's role on issues like climate control and immigration. Pundits on both sides of the political fence saw this move as problematic. Individuals like Cornel West press the president when they assert, as West did: "You don't play with Martin Luther King Jr. and you don't play with his people. By his people, I mean people of good conscience, fundamentally good people committed to peace and truth and justice, especially the Black tradition that produced it."[4] West made these comments about the inauguration as a protest to Obama seeking to place himself in the tradition of King. West believes Obama has not and is not doing enough to address the ills facing African Americans.[5]

Pressing from a different direction are individuals like Senator Rand Paul who, in response to how his inaugural speech would have been differed from President Obama's stated: "Well, instead of Hugo Chavez, you might hear references to Madison and Jefferson. I know he didn't actually literally refer to Chavez, but he referred to a lot of liberal policies."[6] Rand was disturbed that Obama did not place himself in the *right* tradition and was doing too much for the dispossessed.

We seek to navigate this impasse by examining whether it is possible to move beyond self-evident rights to self-executing rights. To this end, we turn to the Trayvon Martin case to explore these rights. Second, we briefly outline one of the ways King sought to help African Americans experience life, liberty, and the pursuit of happiness more fully. Third, we explore how Obama parallels King's insights on moving toward a fuller humanity. Finally, we address the issue of self-executing rights and the reality of true liberation for all individuals.

## Trayvon Martin

Trayvon Martin was visiting his father in Sanford, Florida, when he walked to a store on February 26, 2012. George Zimmerman, a neighborhood watch captain, noticed Martin, an African American male dressed in a black hoodie, and called 911 to report a suspicious person in the neighborhood.[7] Martin's race, and perhaps to some extent his attire, was the basis for Zimmerman's call.

The 911 operator told Zimmerman "not to get out of the car or to approach the individual."[8] Zimmerman ignored the instructions and confronted Martin.[9] No one is sure what occurred during the confrontation. We know that Martin was talking to a friend who heard him ask Zimmerman, "Why are you following me?"[10] People heard screams and shots, after which, Martin was dead!

Though not initially charged for Martin's death, when Zimmerman was taken into custody[11] an officer verified he was bleeding from his nose and the back of his head.[12] Following an initiative launched initially by Rev. Al Sharpton on behalf of Trayvon Martin's parents, Zimmerman was charged with second-degree murder. At issue in this trial was Florida's Stand Your Ground legislation. While not explicitly used as a defense strategy, defense attorneys portrayed Martin as the one followed and turned aggressor rather than a citizen exercising his right to self-defense. In addition, in her pre-deliberation instructions to the jury, Judge Nelson stated that, "they should acquit Zimmerman if they found he had no duty to retreat and had the right to stand his ground and meet force with force, including deadly force if he reasonably believed that it was necessary."[13] In other words, through a selective use of terminology, the judge conveyed to the jury Zimmerman's right to stand his ground and defend himself if he felt threatened, irrespective of the fact that it was he who was in pursuit with a gun, not Martin.

Another Florida case involving the Stand Your Ground law adds perspective to the Zimmerman stand your ground defense. Marissa Alexander, a mother estranged from her husband Rico Gray, suffered a history of domestic violence at his hands.[14] Multiple accounts about what occurred on the day of their altercation include Alexander's actions. Gray, reportedly upset after he discovered text communication between his wife and her first husband,[15] issued a threat which Alexander took seriously.[16] Gray tried to block Alexander from getting out of the bathroom, but she managed to get out and went to the car to get her gun.[17] She returned and told Gray to leave. When he refused, she fired a warning shot in the air.[18] Gray ran out of the front door.[19]

Alexander sought to use the stand your ground law as defense, as Zimmerman did. But the judge rejected a motion by Alexander's attorney to grant her immunity under the stand your ground law. According to the judge's order, the defense lacked sufficient evidence to merit use of this law. The fact that Alexander came back into the home instead of leaving suggests she did not face imminent danger. Alexander was sentenced to 20 years in prison, not for killing her husband, but for firing a warning shot.

In response to the judge's ruling, Florida State Representative Corrine Brown said "that if women who are victims of domestic violence try to protect themselves, the 'Stand Your Ground Law' will not apply to them...The second message is that if you are black, the system will treat you differently."[20] Brown was confused on how the law could apply to Zimmerman but not apply to Alexander.[21] Does she not have a right to defend herself?

We are not legal experts. Perhaps there are legal reasons why stand your ground applies in one case and not the other,[22] but it is still problematic that Alexander could not use this defense. At question in both cases is an issue of rights and whose rights are being protected. In the Zimmerman case, the judge instructed the jury that Zimmerman had a right to defend himself, and with force if necessary. In the Alexander case, the judge ruled that stand your ground is not applicable. The circumstances in the Alexander case include a history of domestic violence and life-threatening warnings by her estranged husband. Zimmerman, on the other hand, had no prior history with Martin and was explicitly told by the 911 operator not to pursue the boy, yet was permitted to use the stand your ground law as part of his defense.

Self-evident rights and self-executing rights in these cases lead to a very different conclusion than that proffered by President Obama in his 2013 inaugural speech. As Obama asserted,

> We recall that what binds this nation together is not the colors of our skin or the tenets of our faith or the origins of our names. What makes us exceptional—what makes us American—is our allegiance to an idea, articulated in a declaration made more than two centuries ago: "We hold these truths to be self-evident, that all men are created equal, that they are endowed by their Creator with certain unalienable rights, that among these are Life, Liberty, and the pursuit of Happiness." (Barack Obama, "President Obama's Inaugural Address," January 21, 2013)

Alexander and Martin's family did not think that the right to life, liberty, and the pursuit of happiness were self-evident. In fact, many would argue that Martin's loss of life did not receive the justice that was due because these rights are not self-evident for all Americans. Race and gender play a role in how evident these rights are for individuals. In both cases, what seems self-executing is that African Americans, and particularly African American women, do not enjoy life, liberty, and the pursuit of happiness in the same manner as others.

What is self-evident in the United States is that rights do not equate to liberation in the fullest sense of the word. James Cone commented in the twentieth anniversary edition of *A Black Theology of Liberation*, "I assumed that if blacks were creatively integrated into all aspects of American society, the issue of racism would essentially be solved. This was a faulty analysis, because I failed to see that the problem of the human condition involved much more than simply the issue of racism."[23]

As Cone pointed out, to equate liberation with fitting into society is faulty. Liberation should be about seeking full humanity and not simply fitting into a preconceived ideal of society. What is self-executing is that to be human one must fit into this round hole even if she or he is a square peg. Alexander and Martin did not fit into this prescribed round hole so justifications are created for denying their rights of life, liberty, and the pursuit of happiness.[24] Alexander and Martin are examples in the news, but others experience the same oppression of their rights daily. How do we deal with this chasm between self-evident and self-executing rights? In his speech Obama stated,

"Today we continue a never ending journey to bridge the meaning of those words with the realities of our time."[25] The reality is individuals like Martin and Alexander do not experience life, liberty, and the pursuit of happiness as self-executing and may not believe they are self-evident. Is this a claim we can or even should make?

## Where Do We Go from Here?

Toward the end of his life, King struggled with the relevancy of life, liberty, and the pursuit of happiness as self-evident concepts for African Americans. In part, for King, the struggle was about the direction the civil rights movement would take going forward. In the second chapter of *Where Do We Go from Here,* King recalls discussions with Stokely Carmichael about the use of the phrase "Black Power."[26] For King, the debate hinged, ultimately, on the message that was to be conveyed.[27] Eventually, though he perceives it as "a reaction to the failure of white power,"[28] King concedes that Black Power was a part of the movement's nomenclature. According to F. Douglas Powe, for King, the fact that this term was necessary meant a continued division between blacks and whites that detracted from moving toward rights together. King understood this reality, but still hoped for a brighter future for African Americans to experience life, liberty, and the pursuit of happiness.

We perceive King as providing a vision in *Where Do We Go from Here* as a basis from which to interpret how life, liberty, and the pursuit of happiness can become self-evident for African Americans. A primary concern is whether this vision simply seeks to integrate African Americans into a predetermined definition of humanity. Is it a definition of humanity based on fitting into society, but not necessarily one where African American humanity is valued on its own accord? Or, is it a vision that can alter the way we experience rights in the United States?

King acknowledged many of the challenges that African Americans encountered as they sought basic human rights— United States of American rights. As he noted, "The gap between promise and fulfillment is distressingly wide. Millions of Negroes are frustrated and angered because extravagant promises made little more than a year ago are a mockery today. When the 1965 Voting Rights Law was signed, it was proclaimed as the dawn of freedom and the open door to opportunity."[29] What King articulated is that the passing of the law did not translate into liberation for African Americans. Words on paper did not effect a change in the lived reality of persons who resided in the south and other geographic locations in the United States that practiced a subtler form of Jim Crow.[30] It is fair to say King was not naïve about the circumstances with which African Americans contended and the challenges they would face in the future.

The question then, as it is now, is: "How to respond?" King perceived three ways to respond that might promote a healthier human condition. First, King suggested African Americans must develop a somebodyness.[31] For King, it was important that African Americans understand their human worth.[32] A history of slavery, Jim Crow and oppressive practices in the United States legally denied the human worth of African Americans.[33] Garth Baker-Fletcher described King's understanding of somebodyness as "a traditional Christian view of human beings in which every person is created in the image of God."[34]

To deny African Americans their humanity is to deny that they are children of God. Those who are denied their human worthiness almost always have a desire to regain it because in doing so they are liberated.[35] A key component of this liberation is a "desegregated mind."[36] This is a mind that is not chained to the way things are in society, but a mind that starts to live as if liberation is a reality now.[37] The reality is long after physical freedom is gained those who have been oppressed are trying to free the chains on their minds.

Somebodyness is a means by which one can counter mental chains placed upon African Americans by society. It is claiming to be a child of God in the midst of the harshest oppression. It is African Americans' ability to see themselves as fully made in God's image irrespective of how others choose to define them. Baker-Fletcher suggested that King believed when African Americans embrace the ideal of somebodyness, this very sense of personal and communal self-understanding would restructure relationships in society. Baker-Fletcher wrote,

> King envisioned life as a piano with both black and white keys, where *all* the keys would be valued for their contribution in producing the harmonious music of living together. King believed that if Blacks would gain the genuine self-appreciation and self-acceptance of Somebodyness, a process could begin whereby white Americans might come to understand integration as "an opportunity to participate in the beauty of diversity."[38]

Somebodyness is not simply about individual African Americans developing a sense of worth. Rather, it is about moving society toward a new way of being together. A way of being together that values all as made in the image of God.

Second, King believed that African Americans needed to work to construct a positive group identity.[39] Here King sought to distinguish between group isolation and group unity.[40] Isolation is retreating to one's own group and not believing other groups should be involved in the fight for rights. For instance, at the planning for the Meredith, Mississippi march some argued, "This should be an all-black march."[41] This is the attitude of isolation that King confronted and sought to distinguish from group trust and unity.

For King, the move toward trust and unity was about a new self-image for African Americans.[42] It is about African Americans being reconciled to themselves in a way that promotes high human ideals—life, liberty, and the pursuit of happiness. King was clear that it was not about uniformity.[43] It is not about suppressing differences or the expression of those differences, but understanding the importance of respecting the basic humanity of all, even in our differences.

Cone described what King alluded to in the following manner, "it is clear from divine revelation as witnessed in Scripture that authentic liberation of self is attainable only in the context of an oppressed community in the struggle of freedom."[44] In other words, we must define liberation based on our sisters and brothers experiences. While anyone of them is in bondage it means we all suffer a loss of life, liberty, and the pursuit of happiness.[45] The notion of group trust and unity is centered on an understanding that my humanity is tied to your humanity. We cannot be liberated until everyone is liberated.

The focus on group trust and unity is about finding ways to elevate African American humanity together, without isolating ourselves from other groups. For example, King expressed his appreciation for the Nation of Islam's commitment to help those often overlooked (e.g., excons), but challenged their separatist mentality.[46] A primary goal and challenge is to be reconciled to one another as African Americans as we seek simultaneously to be reconciled to Anglos. King admitted this is a "complex and monumental" task.[47]

Third, King argued African Americans "must make full and constructive use of the freedom [they] already possess."[48] By this King means not waiting for some future time to live as citizens of the United States, but doing so right now.[49] For King, this was about African Americans individually and collectively giving their talents to the nation.[50] Although King did not state it in this way, the thinking is that giving our talents for the betterment of society will not only increase our self-image, but also the image of others toward us.

The other aspect, possessing freedom now, emphasizes how African Americans can build toward a more liberated future. King admitted that some of the older African Americans in the community were scared of a different future because of the scars of oppression.[51] If, however, some of the younger individuals in the community contributed their talents, King surmised things could change and liberation would become a reality.

King's argument in this instance is reminiscent of Du Bois' the talented tenth.[52] Reminiscent in the sense that a group of individuals within the community will be the ones who move us forward based upon their contributions to society. The fact that King lists individuals like Booker T. Washington and George Washington Carver who achieved such a status in society gives credence to this claim. Liberation in this context is a move to integrate into the culture, albeit white, of the United States.

Certainly we have not captured the entirety of King's argument for moving African Americans toward fuller humanity. This concise overview does, however, provide a base line from which to understand his emphasis on transformation as not incompatible with integration into society. For King, somebodyness, group unity, and taking possession of liberation now are all a means to help African Americans achieve full humanity while realizing the United States of America's ideal of life, liberty, and the pursuit of happiness. For some, the strength of King's argument is his challenge of systemic oppression without necessarily dismantling core values articulated in the Declaration of Independence. In his 2013 inaugural address, President Obama picks up on some of King's themes and seemingly seeks this same balance. It is to his address we now turn our attention.

## Obama

As we pointed out at the beginning of this chapter, the premise of Obama's 2013 inaugural address was that life, liberty, and the pursuit of happiness are self-evident, but not always self-executing. An essential goal of his address was to help those in the United States think about how these self-evident rights can become self-executing. We contend that Obama's basic argument resonates with King's. In his speech, Obama claimed the way to make life, liberty, and the pursuit of happiness self-executing is to follow King's blueprint.

Obama picked up on the theme of somebodyness in his address as key to rights becoming self-executing. Obama stated, "We are true to our creed when a little girl born into the bleakest poverty knows that she has the same chance to succeed as anybody else, because she is an American; she is free, and she is equal, not just in the eyes of God but also in our own."[53] One of the keys for King was that somebodyness meant being made in the image of God. Obama picked up on this ideal and extended it to all Americans.

For Obama, the rights of life, liberty, and the pursuit of happiness are not only God given rights, but also rights that we are called to uphold as citizens of the United States. What the forty fourth president implied was that it is our willingness to consistently uphold these rights that will transformed them into self-executing rights. All individuals in the United States, regardless of whether they were born in the worst conditions or best, will experience life, liberty, and the pursuit of happiness. Every US citizen is somebody and by upholding the self-evident rights of the "founding fathers," who were initially inclusive, although the Declaration of Independence was not, in meaning and application, these rights can become self-executing.

Obama also picked up on the theme of constructing a positive group identity. He differed from King's articulation of the theme with his focus on an "American identity." Obama stated, "We, the people, still believe that our obligations as Americans are not just to ourselves, but to all posterity."[54] Obama proposed there is something constructive that can happen when we move beyond individualistic views and value our collective American citizenry.

Obama expressed a collective concern for our sisters and brothers that invites us to see and acknowledge their humanity. That is why he quips, "We do not believe that in this country freedom is reserved for the lucky, or happiness for the few."[55] Obama believes we are all in this together and that freedom is a right of every citizen. Although Obama did not say this explicitly, it means a sacrifice by those with more to make sure all US citizens enjoy basic freedoms. While Obama's focus is broader than King's, the ideal of a constructive unity based upon concern for all is still foundational to his notion of the common good.

Obama, like King, desires we possess these rights now. Obama asserted, "That is our generation's task—to make these words, these rights, these values of life, and liberty and the pursuit of happiness real for every American."[56] Obama's point is that women should earn equal wages, gay brothers and lesbian sisters should be treated equitably, and people should not have to wait hours to vote.[57] Obama believes that the current generation has the ability to make these rights self-executing and not simply self-evident.

Obama tries to differentiate between the possessing of these rights now and debates over government's role in rights.[58] Obama challenges individuals to make sure life, liberty, and the pursuit of happiness are things all people can experience. He does not suggest that this generation will settle the debate over government's role related to those rights. Even as debates occur on the government's role in society, this should not affect the way individuals experience self-evident rights.

While Obama's remarks were not focused on African Americans, it is easy to see parallels between his address and King's insights into blacks' experiencing fuller humanity. In both cases, the underlying goal is to develop a stronger citizenry for the United States. King wanted African Americans to enjoy the full rights of citizenship like their Anglo brothers and sisters. Obama desires that all enjoy the highest ideal that defines citizenship in the United States. Obama stated, "You and I, as citizens, have the power to set this country's course. You and I, as citizens, have the obligation to shape the debates of our time—not only with the votes we cast, but with the voices we lift in defense of our most ancient values and enduring ideals."[59] These ideals are not only about experiencing a fuller humanity, but about what it means to be a citizen in the United States of America. On the surface, it seems like this is the sort of speech, given its commitment to a fuller humanity and citizenship in the United States, that would be appreciated by all.

At the beginning of this chapter, we talked about Obama's critiques on both sides of the fence using West and Rand as representatives. Neither side likes the tightrope Obama seeks to walk between those embedded in the King tradition versus those who are committed to the founders of the country, often without a historical cultural nuanced analysis. Following, is one example of how Obama attempted to walk the tightrope, "We, the people, declare today that the most evident of truths—that all of us are created equal—is the star that guides us still; just as it guided our forebears through Seneca Falls, and Selma, and Stonewall; just as it guided all those men and women, sung and unsung, who left footprints along this great Mall, to hear a preacher say that we cannot walk alone; to hear a King proclaim that our individual freedom is inextricably bound to the freedom of every soul on Earth."[60] Obama seeks to recognize the foresight of those who constructed an ideal and those who sought to make it a reality for all.

West criticizes Obama for not going far enough in exercising the power of his office to seek justice on behalf of the downtrodden. West has been a consistent critic of Obama and the inaugural address is no exception. West stated, "The righteous indignation of a Martin Luther King, Jr. becomes a moment of political calculation. And that makes my blood boil."[61] West's assessment suggests that Obama is not committed to liberation and simply uses King for political grandstanding. Is this a fair critique given the way King articulates the ideal? What King proposed was a way of being in the world that promotes one's humanity. Obama picked up on this theme and frames the challenge such that it is the responsibility of all citizens to promote human rights. Is Obama simply doing this for political grandstanding or is he committed to these ideals? It is impossible to answer this question in an absolute fashion. West may wish for Obama to take more direct action, but it is probably not entirely fair to suggest the address is simply political calculation.

Rand criticized Obama for not sticking with those who were the constructors of the ideals of rights. Rand seems to be indicating that Obama is negating the purity of the principles by highlighting others who sought to live out and experience these rights. For example, Obama references King in the address.[62] Is this a fair critique given the way we interpret such principles? Obama takes a principle dear to many and illustrates how it has been lived out and can be lived out in ways to make sure all are perceived as citizens. Rand, of all people, is interested in a strong citizenry and a smaller role for government. Obama seems to be highlighting a way to execute what Rand and others who share his beliefs continuously promote—it is about strong citizenship.

What both West and Rand miss is Obama's attempt to hold together two traditions that are often diametrically opposed to each other politically. Obama uses the values this country was allegedly built upon—life, liberty, and the pursuit of happiness—to illustrate how it is possible for these traditions to be held together. The point is that although these two traditions are in tension with one another, it is possible to hold them together. This seems to be the crux of Obama's speech and it was the foundation of King's ideals. The question remains can these rights be self-executing for individuals like Martin and Alexander who seemingly were on the wrong end of enjoying full human rights?

## Self-Executing

The word self-executing is interesting in terms of rights. The basic meaning is something that is in effect without outside help. In other words, life, liberty, and the pursuit of happiness should be rights that are experienced by all US citizens without any outside influence. Of course Obama's point is that life, liberty, and the pursuit of happiness are perceived rights (evident), but they should be rights that one has without having to consciously do anything to experience them. Certainly we do not believe Obama is claiming that these rights will just magically be in effect without work on our part. The question is, "What kind of work and to what extent will these rights be in effect for all?"

Although many individuals are suspicious of starting with the bible, it is, for F. Douglas Powe, a starting point in this case. In Matthew 26:11, Jesus tells the disciples, "The poor you will always have with you, but you will not always have me."[63] Jesus utters these words after a nameless woman anoints him with expensive oil that the disciples deem a waste of resources. Rather than focus on the use of the oil deemed by some as a valuable resource, we emphasize the insight by Jesus that the poor will always be with you.

In many ways, this is a troubling and challenging insight that the poor will always be with us. If we take Jesus' insight seriously, and we should given the reality of history, then those who do not experience life, liberty, and the pursuit of happiness will always be with us. This means for some these rights will never be self-executing in the sense of being in effect without outside influence. The truth is for some they will not be in effect at all. It seems Obama's ideal of humans experiencing these rights is faulty because these rights will never be self-executing for all.

While it may be prudent to make that case, it is not the one we wish to make. Obama's and King's perspective can be critiqued on several levels, but our focus, given the reality of those not experiencing life, liberty, and the pursuit of happiness as a possibility, is whether we can really move beyond these rights being self-evident. We believe this is the crux of what both Obama and King address. In other words, "Can these rights be more than words on paper?"

Cone helps us, theologically, to understand the issue pressed by Obama and King in terms of liberation. Cone believes understanding liberation requires differentiating between universal human nature and black concreteness.[64] For Cone, the challenge is a tendency to universalize the human condition in such a way that the concreteness of the black experience disappears. For example, Alexander and Martin are not victims of an unjust system that favors Anglos, but are simply humans caught in unfortunate circumstances. Cone believes the latter is a misinformed understanding of existence and one that perpetuates oppression.[65]

Cone is adamant that, "God did not become a universal human, but an oppressed Jew."[66] God became a concrete human being in human history not as one of the oppressors, but as one of the oppressed. We should not take this for granted in thinking about what it means to be human. We should not take this for granted in thinking about human freedom. Our understanding of humanity should always be connected to what it means for the oppressed to experience liberation.[67]

The key is liberation is not a freedom to do as one pleases, but it is a deliberate act to stand in solidarity with those who are denied their humanity. This means freedom is defined by participating with the oppressed and not by one's ability to do as one pleases.[68] For Cone, we can only understand liberation from the perspective of the oppressed. In the Alexander and Martin case the question is, "Who is oppressed?" Alexander's estranged husband and Zimmerman also believe their rights were being denied. They would not necessarily disagree with Cone, and would place themselves in the role of oppressed.

Cone countered this perspective by arguing the issue is not that individuals like Zimmerman are not oppressed the issue is their participation on behalf of the oppressor.[69] Cone wrote, "The oppressed become objects to be used to make the world more amenable to the whims of the masters."[70] Zimmerman perpetuates a constructed reality in the United States perhaps not fully understanding he is doing so. Cone's point is siding with the oppressed is not as easy as it seems because the structures in place push us toward participating with the oppressor.

Certainly Cone's perspective illumines why the poor are always with us, but not necessarily the hope we find articulated by Obama and King. Obama and King are aware of the reality to which Cone speaks and yet they still have hope for humanity. Cone can also help us to understand this hope and the possibility of experiencing full humanity. For Cone, it is a dialectical hope and not simply one of having rights. It is a dialectic between liberation and oppression.

As stated in the above paragraphs, to be free is to participate with the oppressed.[71] This dialectic is central to black liberation theology because it defines the way in which humans are to relate to each other and understand their relationship to God. For Cone, to be made in the image of God is not simply about a personal relationship with God. Quite the contrary, the *imago Dei* is a relationship that defines the meaning of human freedom.[72] Therefore, no human is free or experiences completely the image of God until all humans are liberated from oppression.

It is this dialectic that should challenge us and give us hope as Christians. It is in fact true that being made in God's image is self-evident. By self-evident we mean that all humans are made in God's image and have a relationship with the divine. What is self-evident is always in tension with the reality of experiencing the fullness of God's image or, to use Obama's term, what is self-executing. Cone described the tension between what is self-evident (being made in God's image) and what is self-executing (experiencing the fullness of the image) as liberation is about both—a relationship with God, and struggle.[73]

As humans, we live with this tension daily. We live knowing that we are God's children, but being God's child does not mean we will not struggle. As Christians, we already know the result of the struggle because in Jesus full humanity was experienced. This means our struggle to experience liberation is not in vain! Those who are oppressed can live as if they are experiencing liberation now even as they struggle.[74] By experiencing liberation now, we do not mean in the form of escapism, but as one who knows current circumstances cannot define a sense of personal being.

Neither King nor Obama explicitly expressed their hopes for rights in dialectical fashion. Yet, if we interpret their perspectives in this manner, it can open up a new possibility to understand self-executing. Self-executing does not have to mean it is in place right now. However, understood dialectically, it can mean living with the tension between what is self-evident and executing. The right to life, liberty, and the pursuit of happiness may be self-evident, but these rights are always in tension with the reality of those who continue to struggle to experience fully these rights. It also means that until all experience these rights, none of us have these rights. This is the paradox to which Cone points.

If we think dialectically, then we can also see the Martin and Alexander cases in a different light. We no longer think in terms of how something like this can happen in the twenty first century. Instead, we should realize the struggle toward full humanity is on-going even as we live as though those rights are fully embodied now. These cases are reminders that postracial talk and other such conversations are premature. The tension between what is and what ought to be is an ongoing struggle in which we actively participate.

The point is, none of us should get comfortable and think we have life, liberty and are pursuing happiness. It is not about what we experience as an individual. As long as situations like Martin and Alexander's continue to exist, none of us are free. While life, liberty, and the pursuit of happiness may be self-evident rights, the struggle to fully embody those rights continues and we are called to be informed participants in this collective struggle.

In response to the Zimmerman verdict, Obama alluded to the dialectic as a framework for how to understand race. Obama posited, "Each successive generation seems to be making progress in changing attitudes when it comes to race. It does not mean we are in a postracial society. It does not mean that racism is eliminated."[75] Reading between the lines, Obama implied the struggle is ongoing and we should not believe we have made it.

Near the end of the speech he articulated that dialectic well when he suggested that, "we're becoming a more perfect union—not a perfect union, but a more perfect union."[76] One could argue that the verdict altered Obama's view and that he is less positive than he was six months earlier when he delivered his inaugural address. We also think it is possible that even in his inaugural address Obama realized the ongoing nature of the struggle and that we are called to participate so that all may experience life, liberty, and the pursuit of happiness. Certainly his speech in the aftermath of Trayvon Martin's death and his killer's acquittal makes this perspective plainer. At the same time, Obama's hopes were and are that we will struggle together toward a perfect union. King's hopes were that we would struggle together toward a beloved community. In both cases the hopes imply a dialectic between what is and what ought to be. In both cases, life, liberty, and the pursuit of happiness are self-evident, but not self-executing until all experience these rights in their lives.

Earlier we pointed out that Obama aims to hold a King tradition in tension with a founding "father's" tradition. Many of the president's critics oppose this approach because they want him to favor one tradition over the other. Given Cone's analysis, Obama attempts to help individuals live with the reality that those without life, liberty, and the pursuit of happiness are always with us. His insights about the human condition lead him to conclude this is an ongoing struggle in which we are called to participate. It is our application of these rights that move us toward a more embodied experience of life, liberty, and the pursuit of happiness.

# 4

# The World House: Reclaiming the Dream of Dr. King in the Age of Obama

Competing religio-political narratives in the United States of America have continued, to the present time, to appear throughout the history of this country's theo-drama. From the fragile days of the American War of Independence where Thomas Paine, on the eve of signing the Declaration of Independence, said "these are the times that try men's souls" till now, there is something powerful happening in our world today. It is as if a new world is coming into being, a world of difference and plurality, where the bonds of slavery and bondage are breaking and old limitations are transforming into new possibilities. Forging a religio-political narrative that meets the challenges of a global world, a world of difference, and plurality, means calling upon prophetic voices that offer an inclusive and expansive vision for today and tomorrow. The life and legacy of Dr. Martin Luther King Jr., particularly his concept of the "World House" serves as a compelling exemplar of peace, justice, reconciliation, and community for today's world. In the age of Obama, it would seem that advancing Dr. King's dream and legacy is perhaps even more urgent now than ever before.

The world was watching when the first black president of the United States of America, Barack Hussein Obama, took the oath of office for a second historic turn. To win in 2008 was a miraculous fete in and of itself, but to win again in 2012 was not only miraculous it may even be divine. The historic nature of Obama's second inauguration in Washington, DC, does not make sense apart from the long struggle for freedom and human dignity, from sorrows of our enslaved African ancestors who stepped upon these shores more than four hundred years ago in chains, to those who endured over a hundred years of racialized Jim Crow segregation, and yes even now millions living in the shadows of history's pain, as the legacy of slavery and Jim Crow can now be felt in the cries of millions impoverished and over a million and a half blacks in jails and prisons across the nation.

The irony of President Obama's second inauguration is that it occurred on the same day that the United States of America commemorated Dr. Martin Luther King Jr. The year 2013 marks the fiftieth Anniversary of the March on Washington and the historic "I Have A Dream" speech.[1] It also marks the one hundred and fiftieth Anniversary of the signing of the Emancipation Proclamation. Both events set in motion an unfolding drama of freedom and justice, a drum-beat of human dignity marching through history like a mighty army. Dr. King delivered the "I Have A Dream" speech on August 28, 1963, during a year that perhaps depicts the fiercest struggles of the civil rights movement.

Coming just off the heels of the Freedom Rides of 1961, when students from across the north and north-east boarded buses and rode across the south protesting, challenging, and dismantling segregation laws, with leaders now turning their attention from segregated lunch counters to voting rights, Dr. King and his leaders descended on Birmingham, Alabama (what some called Bombingham). It was there that King wrote the famed *Letter from Birmingham Jail* on strips of tissue paper, where he proclaimed that "injustice anywhere is a threat to justice everywhere" and that it is the responsibility of all of us to stand up for justice, freedom, and equality, wherever we see injustice in the world.[2]

That same passionate determination led Dr. King to speak out against the war in Vietnam and then to introduce the

Poor People's Campaign where he would organize the poor people of the nation to establish a Bill of Rights for the Poor as an amendment to the Constitution of the United States of America. On the days leading up to his April 4, 1968, assassination, King was scheduled to preach at Ebenezer Baptist Church, his home church, in Atlanta, Georgia. Instead, he traveled to Memphis, Tennessee, to meet with striking sanitation workers to discuss their plans to march. The mood was tense and the atmosphere violent. King's friends in the movement warned him not to go. But because of his commitment to the cause, he went. Although he was tired, he went out to the Masonic Temple and delivered what we now know as the great "Mountaintop" speech.

In what would be his last speech, King concluded, "but it really doesn't matter with me now, because I've been to the mountaintop."[3] "Like anybody (he said), I would like to live a long life, longevity has its place... but I'm not concerned about that now and he's allowed me to look over and I've seen the promised land."[4] Even as his countenance changed, with a glare of powerful determination and resolution, he said "I may not get there with you, but we as a people will get to the promised land." "I'm not fearing any man, mine eyes have seen the glory of the coming of the Lord."[5]

And now as we reflect 50 years later on Dr. King's dream, life, and legacy, it is as if we can see his dream unfolding. That bursting into being is the Kin-dom of God, the making of a new heaven and a new earth, and though it has yet to be realized fully, it seems as though we can see glimpses of the power and brilliance of God's new world being made possible.

Hill, in particular, resonates with this unfolding of King's dream on a personal level. Like Sims, he was raised in the belly of the South. He reflects on the fact that he grew up poor but loved. Like the men in Memphis, Hill's father was a sanitation worker. So in a real sense, Dr. King was marching for men like Hill's father, who did the hard work of removing the waste from homes and ensuring clean neighborhoods and communities. Men who did the work no one else wanted to do, the bottom of the barrel dirty but necessary work of society. Hill recalls there were days that he would join his father as he worked and saw the filth and grime of raw sewage circulating at the plants, the smell too horrid to bare, yet Hill's father and his coworkers engaged their work with dignity and grace.

What we find so compelling about the legacy of Dr. King is that he stood with the least of these and the lowliest of these, those whom, as Howard Thurman said, stand with their "backs against the wall"; who struggle everyday with the threat of nihilism and homelessness and despair. During the most heated moments in the movement, King would encourage his followers to live by conviction and purpose for a greater cause. Now, more than ever before, with the rise of drug activity in our communities, where drug selling and incarceration have become a normative pattern of life; where sisters are forced to sell their bodies to feed their children; where it is harder to go to college than to go to jail, it is time to stand up and reclaim a legacy of standing and sitting, singing and marching, shouting and crying, to make this world a better place for our time and generations to come.

We have to keep fighting on these interrelated issues. We must stand up to the National Rifle Association (NRA) and other gun peddlers to proclaim God's way of peace and justice in the world. The NRA is an organization that for decades has been committed not only to upholding the Constitutional right to bear arms, but it also has particularly been committed to advancing a very conservative agenda of privatization and state rights. The NRA has also forcefully promoted deregulation and reduction of government benefits for some of the most vulnerable members of our society. The use of violence and gun ownership celebrated by the NRA has been reflected in their support of more guns as a means to resolve many of the gravest problems of our society. While the NRA has often aligned itself with the religious right, it is quite ironic that a Christian narrative espouses a very different stand—one of peace and nonviolence. In Matthew 26:52, Jesus told Peter, when he lifted the sword to strike the Roman soldier in the Garden of Gethsemane, "Peter, no—for those who live by the sword will die by the sword."[6] Guns in the hands of children and young people are destroying our communities. No child grows up wanting to naturally hurt another human being with a weapon but because of access to guns and the absence of feeling safe in their own homes, they are led into a spiral of violence and trauma. It is time for people of faith to stand up and say God is not pleased, that the Kindom of God is an unfolding of peace and justice breaking into the world.

It is essential to move swiftly in support of Obama on immigration reform and a pathway to citizenship. Now we are aware there are multiple views on this issue about a desired course of action, but immigrants from all backgrounds come to this nation, often escaping poverty and violence in their own countries, seeking a better life for their families. The current laws on immigration are two tiered—one for those with money and the other for those without money. For poor immigrants, it is virtually impossible to go through the legal process, even if they have a job and have demonstrated that they are law-abiding residents. Martin Luther King Jr. reminded us in the *Letter from Birmingham Jail* that some laws are unjust and out of harmony with God's eternal law. A just law is a law that lifts up and affirms human dignity, while an unjust law undermines the inherent dignity of a human being. The current immigration laws are unjust and must be changed.

Truly, now is the time and now is our time to change the current system of mass incarceration that simply warehouses human beings and through the rise of private for profit prisons has erected a sign stating "human beings for sale." It has become the new Jim Crow—a new form of slavery that breeds on petty street crimes of poor communities with no jobs, no hope, and no love. Instead, we must introduce sweeping change toward "restorative justice" that allows more room for courts to let communities be more involved in a process that includes alternative and reentry programs as well as preventative measures, in lieu of fixed sentencing rules. It can be done, it must be done, and God is calling us to this work now in our time. Indeed, these issues are interrelated and connected to a matrix of oppression, related to health care, mental health reform, and that great challenge of poverty that lies underneath it all.

## Reclaiming the Dream

Reclaiming the dream of Dr. King today means doing our part to help make and remake the United States of America into what it can be. While we honor the reelection of President Obama, the fact is that neither he, nor any elected official, can bring about change alone. It is up to each of us now more than ever before to stand up and fight, speak out, march, protest, sing, vote, give, hope, love, read, laugh, cry, and do whatever is necessary so that we might become the change that we seek. Over the next three years, like never before in our lives, we have got to participate in this political process we call a democracy as one way to reclaim Dr. King's dream. We all must do our part.

It is time to work together, across historical barriers of difference, to forge change. Rich and poor, black and white, Christian, Muslim, and Hindu, we must move swiftly toward King's vision of the beloved community that taught us that all life is interrelated. Reclaiming the dream of Dr. King means learning how to lay aside our differences, to hold each other accountable, and to fight for our brothers and sisters in their struggles.

The problem is that we have become much too individualistic today, only concerned about "me, myself, and I." The rise of technology and consumerism has led to isolation and rugged individuality, to the extent that there is a deep and profound distrust that we have toward each other, especially in the black experience. An example of such distrust was observed during the 2008 Presidential election when President Obama's "blackness" was called into question. Whether Obama was "black enough" was a point of major discussion among black activists and intellectuals, or "too black" in mainstream political discourse. At local and state levels, the struggle for black political solidarity continues to be one of the great challenges to advancing the cause of freedom and justice today. In some sense, oppressed and marginalized people have become victims of their own success. But God is calling us to help make way for a new heaven and new earth coming into being, a world where we learn to pursue freedom, justice, and equality as normative practices in the human experience.

We have a great deal of respect for Congressman John Lewis. Almost 22 years after he led six hundred protesters over the Edmund Pettis Bridge on March 7, 1965 to protest voting rights, when Alabama State Troopers on horseback with angry dogs and police clubs began attacking them, he was elected, in 1987, to the United States House of Representatives. Undeterred by violent state sanctioned action, Lewis and his fellow human rights advocates went on to march over the bridge again, then again, with the aid of federal troops. Lewis got his head bashed in, and wears a metal plate in his head to keep his brain in place.

Indeed, with the reelection of President Barack Obama, amid the shadows of widening and deepening gaps between rich and poor across the nation and the world, we are certainly living in a peculiar moment in history. On the one hand, the doors of opportunity appear to be more open than ever before. President Obama's 2008 election signaled a new chapter in the unfolding American theo-drama, representing almost a Zeitgeist (or spirit of the times), as it relates to King's vision of his children one day living in a nation where they would not be judged by the color of their skin but by the content of their character. The signage, even as implementation issues are resolved, of Obama's historic health-care legislation was certainly an expression of that hard fought battle in the war of equality, freedom, and justice.

On the other hand, many are just now beginning to see that the demons of racism, materialism, militarism, and violence have ancient and virulent roots. Their meandering tentacles are as ancient and piercing as the United States itself. The black freedom struggle, steeped in the slave experience, born of freedom's songs and the feet of weary warriors of justice, serves as a fulcrum that makes democracy in the United States intelligible and meaningful in the present moment and into the future. It is in some ways because of the freedom struggle and the desire of the enslaved and their children's children to be free, to live with dignity, justice, and in their full humanity, that the values that the United States upholds in the Constitution are challenged. The historic documents, Constitution, Declaration of Independence and the Amendments to the Constitution, have been tried and tested through the passionate, prophetic, pensive, and persistent struggle to overcome racism, racialized violence, political, economic, psychological, and social dehumanization.[7]

Were it not for the bold and courageous pilgrimage of freedom fighters, both past and present, it is doubtful we would truly understand the words of the Declaration of Independence, when it says, "We holds these truths to be self-evident, that all men are created equal, that they are endowed by their Creator with certain unalienable Rights, that among these are Life, Liberty, and the pursuit of Happiness."[8] While we must avoid any notions of valorizing or justifying the evils of slavery, lynching, American racism, and Jim Crow segregation, the fact is that the struggle for freedom, justice, and equality has helped the United States of America become what it is today and remembering that struggle will dictate the future of this republic as well.

Ralph Ellison, in his April 6, 1970 essay "What America Would Be Like Without Blacks," puts it this way:

> The fantasy of an America free of blacks is at least as old as the dream of creating a truly democratic society. While we are aware that there is something inescapably tragic about the cost of achieving our democratic ideals, we keep such tragic awareness segregated in the rear of our minds. We allow it to come to the fore only during moments of great national crisis.
>
> ...the nation could not survive being deprived of their presence because, by the irony implicit in the dynamics of American

democracy, they symbolize both its most stringent testing and the possibility of its greatest human freedom.[9]

James Baldwin would make a similar observation, with artistic precision as he makes a distinction between whom he is and the ways in which racialization in the United States has cast a certain identity upon him.

In a crowded room of whites, Baldwin looked across the room and said with a kind of veracious and vigilant imagination, "If I am a nigga, you invented me." That is to say the illusion and fiction of black inferiority and white supremacy served as stabilizing narratives in the United States' cultural, political, and religious life, sustaining and perpetuating generations of racialized violence, economic disenfranchisement, and psychological and spiritual trauma. It has been this struggle that Du Bois was referring to in the *Souls of Black Folks* (1903) as blacks were forced to vacillate in the wilderness of double-consciousness, between whom they were (their true nature and being) and who they were compelled to be by virtue of dominating systems of power and white supremacy at work in mainstream society.

The Emancipation Proclamation, as a war measure of Abraham Lincoln, which some historians claim may have turned the tide during the Civil War in the Union's favor, was a major victory in the abolitionist movement. It proclaimed that:

> ...by virtue of the power and for the purpose aforesaid, I do order and declare that all persons held as slaves within said designated states and parts of states are, and henceforward shall be, free; and that the Executive Government of the United States, including the military and naval authorities thereof, will recognize and maintain the freedom of said persons."[10]

These words have resounded loudly over the last one hundred and fifty years, all across the nation, from city to city, and town to town. We are not immigrants. We are descendants of and recipients of the dreams of enslaved and freed persons of color.

Building on what Albert Raboteau called "Slave Religion," a religion steeped in perseverance, faith, hope, and love, we remember the proud full bodied women adorning white dresses standing at the doors, as if awaiting a presidential palace, moving with grace and dignity, as the preacher preached, as if enacting a great theatrical performance, with sweat dripping on aged bibles, amid the frenzied motions of hands waving and bodies in motion like mist over an angry sea.[11] Charles Marsh observed in *God's Long Summer: Stories of Faith and Civil Rights*, that it was the beautiful chaos that shaped and formed the young Dr. King, that chaos that transformed a young Baptist preacher into a global visionary leader and revolutionary for all ages; that inspired leaders all over the world, and that captured the imagination of the young idealistic community organizer by the name of Barack Hussein Obama, inspiring him to dream, sparking the slogan of millions with "yes we can" and "si se puede."[12]

The United States of America is truly at a pivotal moment in human history. We are witnessing the browning and diversification of citizens and the planet, a fluidity of cultures, religions, races, ethnicities, bursting on the face of humanity like never before. Individuals and cultures from around the world are moving beyond their narrow enclaves and interrelating, sharing, talking, loving, living, and hoping together like never before. The forces of technology, social networking, cyberspace, mass marketing, and mass communication, as well as the rise in transcontinental travel are now making possible the emergence of a global civilization, a world of differences, where long held narratives such as white supremacy are now being curtailed and disrupted, dismantled, and eulogized at the cemeteries of ideological history.

Yet the spirit of yesterday's sins still linger. Poverty and social neglect have overtaken our world like a tidal wave. The problem of mass incarceration has created, as noted earlier, a "new Jim Crow," and massive amounts of cultural violence has resulted in a rampage of social, political, and economic anxiety. We not only face fiscal cliffs, but moral and spiritual cliffs as well. Now, during the fiftieth anniversary of the March on Washington and King's "I Have a Dream" speech, there is a more urgent need to reflect on the relationship between the black freedom struggle, President Obama (and subsequently his administration as well), and the legacy of Dr. King.

The fact is that Obama is not King and does not walk in the same trajectory. President Obama is now the face of empire. He is the commander and chief of the most powerful empire that the world has ever known. He was raised by his white grandparents and white mother with a Protestant work ethic informed by their mid-Western roots. The son of a Kenyan, Obama knew very little of his father and an African worldview. His mother imported black culture to him as a child and encouraged him to ground his identity in the songs of freedom and the black freedom struggle. He listened to jazz and blues, the spirituals, and speeches by Dr. King and Malcolm X. He observed his activist mother as she fought for the rights of the poor and marginalized in the streets of Indonesia and Hawaii. Obama also entered the ranks of the elite as a student at Columbia University and later as a law student at Harvard University, where he became editor of the revered Harvard Law Review.

King, on the other hand, was a descendent of the enslaved. Through generational memory and experience, King was handed down a tradition of racial struggle and a quest for freedom. A fourth generation Baptist preacher, he was also steeped in the field of Boston Personalism. Freedom, justice, human dignity, and nonviolence would be his thunderous cries. These cries were heard in these words on the steps of the Lincoln Monument amid the sweltering heat of an August afternoon in 1963, "I have a dream that the sons of former slaves and the sons of former slave owners will be able to join hands and sing in the words of the old negro spiritual—free at last, free at last, thank God almighty, I'm free at last."[13] These words were not simply utterances of a disheveled, insignificant preacher from Sweet Auburn Street in Atlanta, Georgia. They were indeed the sounds of prophetic illumination that may well determine the destiny of humanity.

In these words and the movement that it inspired, they summon that courageous trumpet of community amid difference, the hope for a world without violence or the need for violence, a world of dignity and respect for difference, of love and compassion for neighbor, a world free of poverty and need, where people can be all that God has created them to be. In this particular speech, King spoke of a bad check that the United States had issued to its African descended peoples, a check that "has come back marked insufficient funds."[14] He spoke of the United States living up to its creed and overcoming the voices of those mouths in the south dripping with the "words of interposition and nullification." And yet, he still urged us to dream on a little longer until justice becomes a reality and freedom rings from "every hill and molehill of Mississippi," and "from every mountainside," that it should ring resoundingly until "justice rolls down like waters and righteousness like a mighty stream."[15]

Amid the gaze of history upon us, there are yet and still tasks before us, particularly during these great moments of remembrance, celebration, and hope. Some of those tasks, left undone by history's sorrow, means insisting upon a radical revisitation of the past and to remember rightly! The memory of the past will not go away. It must neither degenerate into mythology nor serve as an occasion for hatred and strife. Rather, it must be revisited as a source of hope and resilience in working toward a better day and a better world. Also, now is the time to build multiracial, multiethnic, and multireligious coalitions to establish dangerous alliances of justice, peace, nonviolence, and reconciliation that will leave a legacy to our children's children, a legacy steeped in coalitions of mutual cooperation and transformation.

The present moment also calls for reclaiming the tradition of radical orthopraxis, where there is a wedding of ideas and action, where theory and praxis merge. That would mean overcoming blind spots of the modern era, a movement that tended to separate thought from actions, perhaps even head from heart. Reclaiming this tradition, a tradition of the spirituals and freedom songs, of marches and radical love, of hope and dignity, can pave a way for others in ways that we could never imagine. It may well help build an expansive, inclusive vision of global justice and difference, where silenced voices speak, the weak are empowered, and the blind are enlightened.

# 5

# When Black Is Not Black Enough

Barack Obama is mixed!
Barack Obama is black!
Barack Obama is not really American because his dad was
  African!

These and similar phrases were spoken throughout the 2008 presidential campaign in an effort to pinpoint then Senator Barack Obama's heritage as though this would determine his stance on racial matters. For many, the issue was not Obama's heritage, but how black is he. In other words, was he Martin Luther King Jr. black or Malcolm X black?[1] Many of then Senator Obama's supporters worked hard to color him in the image of King while several detractors worked hard to connect him to Rev. Jeremiah Wright in an attempt to shade him as Malcolm X black. One underlying motive for painting Obama as Malcolm black is to discredit the ideal that he can be the president for all American citizens. If he is truly a Wright disciple then he is only interested in advocating for African Americans over and against Anglos. Even as many celebrate the election of the United States of America's first African American president, this issue of blackness continues to haunt US culture.[2]

But what is blackness? In other words, who defines this social construction and establishes parameters by which we determine who is or is not categorized as black? Without consideration to biological arguments, many individuals identify their blackness with King or Malcolm X based on their understanding of African American public personas. For instance, Jesse Jackson would identify with King and keeping his dream alive, whereas some perceive Louis Farrakhan as perpetuating Malcolm's dream.[3] In this instance, African American public persona is interpretations of blackness that inform religious, political, and cultural ideals of blackness. It is an ideal that cannot be scientifically verified, but one that catches glimpses of the ways in which individuals understand what it means to be black based on public discourse.

For many African Americans their understanding of blackness is not biological, it is developed in their engagement of religion, politics, and culture. What it means to be prophetic in African American communities often depends on the lens through which one integrates religion, politics, and culture. For example, Andrew Young is perceived as black in a way that is different than Kweisi Mfume.[4] Young marched with King and continued to uphold his ideals, Mfume changed his name from Frizzell Gray to pay homage to his African heritage. Certainly one can ascertain both men are African American by looking at them, but their understanding of blackness was shaped differently because of religion, politics, and culture. Too often, in the United States, because of the way public discourse has occurred, the push is to be black in a certain way—King black or Malcolm X black.

This is one of the challenges Obama faced during the 2008 election. Obama's supporters attempted to paint him as King black.[5] Simultaneously, others attempted to portray Obama as Muslim and associated this religious signification as void of citizenship and thus unqualified to hold the highest elected office in the United States.[6] This way of thinking, which ignores the very plurality upon which this nation was purportedly established, suggests only two options for what it means to be black. There are historical roots for this way of thinking.

Historically, Du Bois' classic definition of blackness as double-consciousness has framed conversations on race for many

African Americans.[7] According to Du Bois, to be African and to be a US citizen is to constantly live in two worlds, whereby one never completely is a part of either.[8] For Du Bois, to be black is to deal with the reality of both black culture and white culture simultaneously. In public discourse this simultaneity often gets translated into an either/or option. One seeks to negate their blackness by taking on the traits of the majority or one seeks to affirm one's blackness by reclaiming one's African heritage.

While Du Bois provides a definition for blackness, he still does not help us to determine whether a litmus test for being black exists. We posit that, right or wrong, in public discourse a litmus test exists. Individuals who pass the test are perceived to be "in" and those who fail are often labeled sellouts. The problem is the litmus test is not written down and is malleable so that no one quite knows the standards on which judgments are based.

Often articulated and lived out dichotomously, some assert that to be black is to have a certain persona. This way of being becomes a standard against which blackness is determined.[9] Because an operating presupposition is that blacks cannot be both African and American, some might assert that Du Bois' sociological analysis as well as James Cone's theological analysis of Martin and Malcolm in the United States is characterized by an identity crisis of duality, that supports a one-dimensional view of African Americans.

If blackness, an identity shared by many US citizens, creates consternation for many as a result of its diverse meanings, it stands to reason that there is more to blackness than being in or a sellout. There are also additional ways, other than those to which we alluded earlier, to understand blackness.[10] The public discourse on blackness, however, tends to be concrete so we will begin, not from a historical point of reference from which to develop an epistemology of blackness but from a contemporary religio-political-cultural framework. This lays the ground-work for a theological analysis of Cone's work and the possibility of a different way forward using Karen Baker-Fletcher's Trinitarian model.

## Public Discourse on Blackness

The meaning of blackness has deep theological roots that under-gird almost all aspects of African American life. While quantita-tive and qualitative data highlight the importance of religion for black life,[11] there is still disagreement on the role religion should play, if any, in defining blackness. One way to understand the contentious aspect of blackness within African American public discourse is to articulate primary differences between prophetic rhetoric and destructive nationalism with specific attention to who determines the distinctive characteristics of rhetoric that is often essential to both an individual and communal identity that is not ahistorical.[12]

The controversy surrounding Rev. Jeremiah Wright[13] focused on differentiating whether he was promoting prophetic rhetoric or destructive nationalism. Although Wright had actively been preaching for over 25 years, his 2008 use of presumed racial-ized language calling into question notions of the United States as a country devoid of national sin set off a political fire storm. For some, Wright's sermonic discourse is prophetic because it is within a tradition of African American prophetic preaching.[14] Others, however, argued Wright was a reverse racist who did not like Anglo people.[15] One way of interpreting these views of Wright is to differentiate between a theological construct of blackness and more general perceptions of race. Certainly interpreting Wright theologically is not mutually exclusive of interpreting race, the difference, in this case, is the lens of inter-pretation for some. Some detractors of Wright only interpret his comments with race in mind.

The Pew Forum, in its report on the above-mentioned issue regarding Wright and black prophetic preaching, indicated that, "For Obama, whose speeches dealt with themes of both race and religion, the press tended to focus on the racial aspects more than the religious ones. In fact, about half (51 percent) of the stories on the speeches were about race while only 1 percent focused on religion."[16] Most media pundits and the general public, many who have neither experiential nor academic knowledge about

African American denominationalism, neglected to interpret Wright's rhetoric theologically, but interpreted it racially. Powe may be correct to suggest that the reason Wright flew under the broader public radar prior to then Senator Obama's presidential campaign can be attributed to a large degree to the fact that his socially informed messages were interpreted within a theological framework.

In an attempt to get to the heart of the issue of Wright's interpretation of blackness, Bill Moyer asked Wright to clarify his understanding of God. Moyer asked, "So, God is not, contrary to some of the rumors that have been circulated about Trinity, God is not exclusively or totally identified with just the black community?"[17] To which Wright responded, "Of course not...God should love the world, not just the black community."[18] Notwithstanding Wright's response in this particular instance and similar responses in other instances, the debate raged on whether his biblical insights were prophetic or simply hurtful race mongering.

By trying to show Wright is anti-white (translated anti-American) and pro-black nationalist, Moyer attempted to discredit the notion that Wright is prophetic. Rather than address historical tensions that inform current realities, Moyer seemed more interested in trying to bait Wright and described his message as destructive to a country trying to move beyond a racial divide.[19] When blackness is defined in an either/or frame, there is often a tendency to see it as either a destructive brand of Black Nationalism, or a more culturally acceptable understanding of race relations. The former suggests that any rhetoric that counters the "American narrative" is politically, religiously, and culturally false. The latter suggest that blackness is absorbed into the "melting pot" myth that is typically associated with the United States.

Politics also define how we understand blackness. Black religiosity always intersects with a political understanding of blackness. For example, some African Americans define blackness based on a political agenda. This, according to Powe, is central to Tavis Smiley[20] and Al Sharpton's[21] ongoing debate about blackness. Smiley believes that Obama's response to an African American political agenda signals that the forty-fourth president is not black enough. Sharpton's response suggests that he deems Smiley's position to be one of exclusivity. After all, as Sharpton stated, Obama is not just the black president but, the president of the entire United States. This exchange underscores the role of race, especially blackness, and its relation to this nation's religio-political narrative. For both Smiley and Sharpton, blackness means a commitment to support African American causes and struggles for true liberation.[22]

Sharpton perceived Obama's commitment to stimulate the economy in general as beneficial for African Americans. Smiley counters that a more specific agenda for African Americans is needed to address ills in the community. He held a summit, "The Black Agenda is the American Agenda," in Chicago on March 20, 2010, to discuss this perspective. Both Smiley and Sharpton are interested in African Americans moving toward liberation but differ, methodologically, on what that means.

What Powe finds interesting is a notion that one's understanding of blackness is shaped by a political agenda that on the surface either portrays you as "for black people (Smiley)" or seemingly satisfied with the status quo (Sharpton). James Taylor suggested this is a debate between power brokers who both vie to be perceived as political and public spokespersons on behalf of all African Americans.[23] Others recognize that this debate, which intensified after the 2008 presidential election, pre-dates Smiley and Sharpton.[24] At issue is a perception that a pro black stance stands in stark contrast to anything that advances the nation as a whole moving forward." In other words, one must deny one's blackness in order to fit into the mainstream of society.

This was one of the political quandaries Obama faced as a 2008 presidential candidate. To be for the greater American good meant he had to distance himself from his pastor. To do otherwise, that is, to maintain a public relationship with Wright, would jeopardize Obama's presidential campaign. Smiley sees this as a pattern, not only with Obama, that dictates a denial of blackness, but also with individuals like Sharpton who seemingly are moving toward assimilation. For Sharpton, Powe posits that blackness is an identity in which clearly distinguishing between blackness and whiteness is not essential. This is not an avowal of blackness, but an understanding that blackness and whiteness are not mutually exclusive. Sharpton views blackness as requisite to one's ability to live up to King's dream of a society where citizens are not defined by social constructions of race. Both Smiley and Sharpton argue for a certain black identity. For Smiley, it is an identity informed by a particular black agenda that focuses on the needs of African Americans. For Sharpton it is an identity that is liberating without negating the other.

When we consider culture, in addition to and in conjunction with religion and politics, a challenge to understand blackness in a particular way intensifies. Because there are many ways to think about the meaning of blackness in African American culture, we elect to focus on music and Afrocentrism as two lenses to interpret expressions of blackness among African Americans.[25]

Regardless of a specific genre, whether rhythm and blues, neo soul, or hip-hop, a tension exists within the African American community between artists who produce black music (which may be read as artists who produce black music in conjunction with record executives, etc.) and those who sell out.[26] To sell out means to make music with a broader mass appeal and to live a life that denies one's heritage. For example, artists like Erykah Badu and The Roots have typically been perceived as making black music.[27] Yet, Will Smith is considered a sellout because of his rap style and stances on issues related to the black community.[28] In black culture, it is a fine line between being black one day and a sellout the next day. There is no logic for who and what determines when one is a sellout. The idea of a sellout is important culturally because it means that there is a preconceived understanding of what it means to be black. An implicit criteria (determining whether one is selling out) for blackness exists that focuses on staying connected to the African American community.[29] A litmus test for staying connected is malleable because there is no established criteria that is applied consistently.

Second, the meaning of blackness is often culturally defined by how Afrocentric one is.[30] By Afrocentric we mean that Africa is the starting point for what it means to be black.[31] An Afrocentric perspective suggests we can only discover the true meaning of blackness by returning to our roots. Afrocentrism gets expressed in various ways in African American culture from attire, art, and education to return-to-the-Motherland-pilgrimages. All of these are an effort to find the true meaning of blackness. It is a search for identity.

The challenge is determining if one is Afrocentric enough. If one wears African attire and collects African art, but ignores the struggles of less fortunate blacks, is this what it means to be black? Certainly these individuals fit the definition of the term, but many would argue that they lack the spirit behind the meaning of blackness. We are not suggesting an Afrocentric lens is inappropriate. Ralph Watkins described the importance of an Afrocentric lens as follows:

> African/African and American ancestry and identity is placed first simply because when I was born into the world I, like you, was assigned a racial category. I was raised in the context of an ethnic heritage that helped define who I was and would become. That racial identity as it was later intertwined with an ethnic reality produced a meta-identity, and it is out of this identity that ethnic groups begin to define themselves as members of the larger society and in relation to a religious tradition.[32]

Watkins argued that we are all shaped by a meta-identity and for African Americans this identity is rooted in various African traditions. Therefore any conversation on what it means to be black is also rooted in our African heritage.

Interestingly, it is Obama's African heritage that contributed to controversy in both the 2008 and 2012 presidential campaigns. Obama's father was from Kenya and many of his detractors claim Obama is not a US citizen, but is African.[33] It is well documented that Obama has gone to Kenya in search of his roots. Given Obama's direct link to Africa and his search for his meta-identity, why is there so much controversy over his blackness? One can argue Obama has a stronger cultural claim to blackness than most African Americans. His detractors argue his cultural ties are not to the United States, but to Africa. His supporters argue because of his mixed heritage Obama epitomizes the American dream. The former suggest his meta-identity is African and perceive this as a negative. The latter suggest his meta-identity is American and subsumes his African heritage underneath what it means to be American.

Defining blackness culturally is just as problematic as defining it politically and religiously. All three themes focus on identity issues. Blackness is defined from particularity (e.g., gangsta persona), but often applied universally to all African Americans. Our epistemological entry into blackness is predicated on developing a persona that is politically, religiously, and culturally shaped by a created mythology. The truth is no one will be black enough to live up to the mythic black persona we have described because an underlying basis for determining blackness often is framed as an either/or option.

This framing of the issue as an either/or option is how many interpret Du Bois' twoness. Either one is black in the ways described above politically, religiously, and culturally, or one buys into Anglo society and denies their blackness. This is a tension African Americans face. This is a tension Obama faced in 2008 and 2012. The focus is on identity and what a black identity means. We now turn to Cone's interpretation of this issue and how he nuances the either/or option.

## Theological Response to Blackness

James Cone is considered by many to be the father of black theology. His early works in particular illumine the issue of black identity. Even decades later Cone still perceives black identity to be a crucial issue. In a plenary discussion at the American Academy of Religion in Montreal, Cone discussed how Malcolm is the black in black theology and Martin the Christian reflection.[34] Cone delineated it in this way to give people a sense of how different aspects of African American culture inform black theology.

Cone suggested by identifying with Malcolm and Martin we discover the true meaning of blackness. He wrote,

> Respect as human beings was the central theme of both Malcolm and Martin in the black freedom struggle. Initially Malcolm believed that "respect" was found primarily in religio-cultural identity—affirming blackness (Africa) and rejecting whiteness (America). By contrast Martin, though he believed black people's cultural identification with Africa was important, contended that blacks could achieve "respect" only by acquiring social and political power in America, as Americans.[35]

For Cone, Malcolm and Martin represent the tension of blackness within the African American community. They illumine Du Bois' concept of double-consciousness in a way that maintains the dialectic between what some perceive as a strong black identity and a more assimilated black identity.[36]

Cone goes on to state that a strong black identity taps into our African heritage and an assimilated black identity is that which gets constructed in the United States. Cone is unique, however, because he offers a theological synthesis that holds these oppositional poles together in his constructive Christology. While African Americans feel the oppositional pull of affirming a particular strand of black identity, Cone argues both are affirmed theologically in Christ, which is what makes the God event so important for African Americans.

It is Cone's move toward a synthesis of these oppositional pulls of black identity that makes his role in the 2008 presidential election so interesting. Some in the media painted Cone's development of black theology as a form of separatism and thus not Christian. For example, in an interview with Hannity and Colmes, Wright argues with them about black theology and the contributions of individuals like Cone.[37] Hannity pushed Wright on his commitment to blackness as expressed on the website of Trinity, by suggesting the descriptions were non-Christian and separatist.[38] Wright responded by contextualizing his use of black as informed by black theology.[39] Hannity continued to push back by suggesting that they talk about King who was interested in bringing Americans together.[40] Hannity's moving of the conversation in this direction indicates he perceives King as doing something different than black theology.

We have only provided snippets of the interview above and it is important that it be read in its entirety, but three themes from this interview that deserve further consideration are the following. First, Cone's synthesis of black identity reframes African American public thinking. Second, Cone grounds his synthesis of blackness in Christ. Third is a critique of Cone's synthesis.

African American public thinking often pushes one to an either/or option. For many African Americans in the United States this has been their interpretative lens for blackness. For example, Powe overheard a conversation between two youth at a summer reading program. The one youth was upset with the other because she was trying to act "white" by using proper English. It is important to note that this is not an anomaly. Many African Americans have experienced or heard these types of comments. This creates a twoness of either in or out and double-consciousness is reduced simply to trying to fit into a certain group rather than serving as an interpretive lens for exploring the richness of African American existence.

A mythology is created that dichotomizes those who are prophetic in a King manner from those prophetic in a Malcolm X manner. To be prophetic in a King manner is perceived as supporting mainstream US ideals (fitting in) and presupposes that blacks can bring about change while integrating into US society.[41] The pre-1965 King (which is the one mainstream tends to idolize because it is before his activism against the Vietnam War) is perceived as furthering the mainstream process even as he speaks out against the way African Americans have been denied access to rights.

Cone suggests King picks up on the universal intent of the phrase "life, liberty, and the pursuit of happiness" as having significance not only for Anglos but also for African Americans.[42] In part, the brilliance of King was his ability to use the tools of the master's house as a means for deconstructing that house. King aimed his public rhetoric at Anglos trying to help them live up to the promise of the American dream.[43] He did this realizing that he offered a counter voice to Malcolm who was perceived as a black nationalistic separatist.

Malcolm X did not shape his rhetoric for Anglo audiences.[44] Malcolm focused on African American audiences and the need for blacks to wake up to their true condition.[45] Unlike King, Malcolm did not perceive the United States' narrative as a dream. Malcolm was not trying to deconstruct the master's house with the master's tools. Malcolm wanted a new house. For Malcolm the goal was not integration into the system, but constructing a true black pride.[46] His prophetic rhetoric was not focused on a universal message, but the particularity of the African American community. Often, in his early years, Malcolm referred to Anglos as the devil.[47] This made Anglos upset and many perceived him to be a black supremacist.[48] Anglos argued Malcolm was a prophet of hate.[49] Malcolm's prophetic rhetoric was based on his interpretation of history and the deeds of Anglos toward people of color.[50] Malcolm reinterpreted the United States' narrative in a way that not only advocated for black dignity but also consistently reminded Anglos of their role in brutalizing African Americans.[51] Because his early prophetic rhetoric was considered anti-American he is identified as the polar opposite of King.

Before moving to Cone's theological synthesis of these messages, it is important to point out how this polarization was manifested in the 2008 election. Wright, because of his sermons and claim to be an advocate for black theology, is perceived to be in the tradition of Malcolm. He is portrayed as a black supremacist. Obama, by eventually distancing himself from Wright, promotes himself as a King-like prophetic voice. Cone believes that many Anglos gravitated to King because he offered hope, whereas Malcolm refused to go this route.[52] Obama ran on a message of hope, a universal message of hope, so that he could not afford to be connected to the kind of prophetic particularity promoted by Wright.[53]

Unfortunately individuals like Hannity, through a cursory engagement with Cone's work, perpetuate an either/or stance and miss the theological synthesis Cone provides as a way to understand blackness. Instead of an either/or choice between King and Malcolm X, Obama and Wright, we contend that emphasis should focus on how these different aspects of black identity inform one another. For Cone, this was expressed in King and Malcolm's commitment to the liberation of African Americans.[54] Both men were committed to helping African Americans develop a new identity of somebody-ness.[55]

Cone proposes that to identify with King does not require that we deny the insights of Malcolm or vice versa. Rather, a more nuanced meaning of blackness can be deduced when we identify with both individuals. Therefore, when Cone writes "Blacks know that there is only one possible authentic existence in this society, and that is to force a radical revolutionary confrontation with the structures of white power by saying yes to the essence of their blackness,"[56] he is not proposing African Americans identify with Malcolm at the expense of King. To say yes to the essence of blackness includes the insights of King and Malcolm.

Cone believes both leaders, each in their own way, forced a "radical revolutionary confrontation" with Anglo power structures. One misinterprets Cone's intent by trying to understand blackness from the perspective of perpetuating a normative reading of the mainstream in the United States. This is precisely where the dialogue falls apart between Wright and Hannity. Wright interprets Cone in a manner that reflects a commitment of black theology to liberation that utilizes insights of both King and Malcolm. Hannity, on the other hand, interprets black theology as a narrow enterprise that opposes a normative reading of the United States' narrative.

To be for blackness is perceived as being against a normative understanding of the American mainstream. The goal is to fit into a preconceived box that calls individuals to forego any identity outside of an "American" identity. In the 2008 election, Obama had to distance himself from Wright so that he could demonstrate to mainstream America that he was not a "black nationalist." Cone argues for a strong black identity as a way to be American. The way Cone synthesizes King and Malcolm promotes a different epistemology, but one that is uncomfortable for many African Americans and Anglos. It is uncomfortable because blackness includes a twoness that counters the status quo. It is a double-consciousness that draws from the insights of black power and black Southern Christianity.

Second, Cone grounds his understanding of blackness in Christology. While Cone used different theological lenses to illumine his perspective, his primary lens is Christology. Cone wrote,

> The definition of Jesus as black is crucial for christology if we truly believe in his continued presence today. Taking our clue from the historical Jesus who is pictured in the New Testament as the Oppressed One, what else, except blackness, could adequately tell us the meaning of his presence today? Any statement about Jesus today that fails to consider blackness as the decisive factor about his person is a denial of the New Testament message.[57]

For Cone, the historical Jesus can only be understood from the perspective of blackness. To be black is to be a part of the oppressed. This means blackness is more than skin complexion because it has to do with a state of being.

It also means blackness is still identity focused. To be black is to be identified with the ultimate symbol of blackness-Christ. Cone argued, "If Christ is not black, then who is he?"[58] The only authentic answer to this question, if we follow Cone's logic, is Christ is black. Cone argued that because Jesus was one of the oppressed (oppressed are black), we must continue to understand Jesus in that same manner today.[59] Without losing sight of Cone's understanding of Jesus as for the oppressed, we push Cone's work in a different direction that focuses more on the deliberations regarding the nature of Jesus. Our premise is that an epistemological lens for interpreting twoness is implicit in Cone's work.

We do not suggest that either King or Malcolm were divine. We focus, instead, on the embodied twoness they represented and how that informs our understanding of blackness. Cone implied a way of interpreting Du Bois that is Christologically grounded in this idea of an embodied twoness. To be black in the United States of America is not a choice between African and Anglo. To be black in the United States is to pay homage to one's African heritage as well as to recognize ways in which we have or are being assimilated into citizens of this republic. African Americans should not perceive one identity as better than the other. Both contribute to the richness of what it means to be an African American in the United States. This is a different epistemological interpretation of blackness than we often hear in popular thinking. Given Cone's focus on Christology, he reinterprets the twoness African Americans experience not as an either/or option, but as an embodiment of a different way to move toward liberation informed by Malcolm and King. A central question for Cone is, "Not am I black, but how am I embodying my blackness?" The heresy is to embody it in a way that is docetic or Arian, privileging one over the other.

A deep engagement of black theology, and particularly Cone, may have helped some during the 2008 presidential campaign to develop a different epistemological lens by which to interpret blackness. It is a lens that challenges the American narrative, but not in destructive ways often portrayed by some. It is a lens that challenges those within African American communities to reconsider their embodiment of blackness, which often falls into Christian heresy. However, before we champion Cone's articulation, it is important to consider some of its shortcomings.

A critique of Cone's synthesis is important for thinking about how to move forward. The challenge is Cone's emphasis on identity. Cone's epistemological synthesis still focuses on identity as the entrée into blackness. To be black is a synthesis of the best of King and Malcolm X. For Christians, in Christ we have the ultimate symbol of the twoness of black identity as expressed in King and Malcolm X. As Cecil Cone wrote more than 30 years ago, "Contemporary problems of identity in the development of Black Theology are directly related to black theologians' rejection of this other-worldly interpretation and their return to Du Bois' political interpretation in order to make common cause with the Black Power Movement."[60] A salient point for our purposes is the capitulation toward identity and in particular political identity as the appropriate epistemological starting point for blackness.

James Cone perpetuates and intensifies this epistemological lens, reducing the ways in which we can understand and ultimately articulate blackness. Secondly, in many cases it makes blackness synonymous with black male identity. For example, someone is King or Booker T. Washington black versus Malcolm X or Du Bois black. Not only is it reductionist for how one understands blackness, it gets reduced to male ways of expressing the meaning of blackness. This is also an epistemological standpoint that negates the ethnic variety of blackness in the United States and also fails to connect with the oppressed around the globe.

Certainly both forms of reduction are perpetuated by a Christological emphasis. If one begins with an androcentric reading of Jesus the Christ, then grounding black identity in Jesus further promotes this issue. Cone avoids the trapping of making twoness an either/or option in the way he develops his understanding of blackness, but he perpetuates other issues related to blackness that reared their head in the last election. In part, this is why Obama and Wright could not escape reductionist categorizations of blackness. The question is, "Is there a way forward that moves the conversation beyond identity?"–

## A Way Forward

A challenge is the way in which both popular thinking and a black theological response continues to frame the issue of blackness in terms of identity. If we are going to shift the epistemological starting point for discussions on blackness, then we have to shift the way it is framed. One way to do this theologically is by moving to a Trinitarian perspective and not simply focusing on Christology. The advantage of this shift is rather than negating identity it reinterprets it, so that it is not the only way of thinking about blackness. In the space remaining we share three ideas that are informed by this movement. First, one begins to think differently about blackness simply by using the language of Trinity. Second, inherent to the notion of Trinity is making space for an other and that allows for multiple expressions of blackness. Third, we offer some closing thoughts on how these theological insights can shift the public discourse.

The language of Trinity expands our understanding of God. God is no longer just understood from a Christological perspective. God becomes the one who is Creator, Redeemer, and Sustainer. God is the one who calls us into relationship with the divine, reconciles us to the divine and then helps to sustain us in that relationship. Simply speaking about God in Christological language reduces the full divinity of God down to a particularity that misses aspects of who God is. To focus only on the reconciling nature of God shortchanges those aspects of God that are creating and sustaining the universe.

When we broaden our language about blackness from a focus on identity to other expressions, it gives us a fuller picture of the meaning of this term. To think about blackness as creating and sustaining, borrowing from Trinitarian language, it expands the way we approach this topic. Blackness is not confined to a particular way of being, but speaks to the way in which African Americans are creating new expressions of blackness while sustaining some older ways. As humans, we cannot dictate the doings of the Triune God or the various ways blackness will be expressed. Karen Baker-Fletcher claims, "The dance of the Spirit belongs to none."[61] Humans do not dictate the expressions of the Spirit. It is not possible to name one way of approaching blackness and claim it as "the way." Blackness is always being created anew, even while we seek to sustain identities and traditions that have gone before us. Obama, in telling his life story, affirms African heritage and his mixed heritage. It is not an either/or choice for Obama. It is moving beyond simple negations that open up the possibility of constructing blackness anew.

The claim that one person is black and another is not is a false claim. Of concern is by what criteria and authority is the claim made. On the other hand, this probably does not mean that every action by an African American points to an aspect of blackness. Defining blackness should be a conversation and not a finger pointing exercise. The goal should not be exclusion, but seeking a deeper understanding and appreciation for what it means to be black.

If we believe no one person or community ever completely understands the Triune God, then it should not be a stretch to believe no one person or community can understand blackness. In describing the challenge of deconstruction and using Jacques Derrida as her example, Baker-Fletcher says, "It is not that there is no reality, human or divine, but that human language is insufficient to name it."[62] Her point about human language being insufficient should be a cautionary note to us all about claiming too much. Yet, she also is clear that it is not an excuse to say nothing.[63] When we speak, we should always be mindful of the claims we are making and for whom we are making the claims.

This is why reframing our language is so critical. We learn more about the persons of the Trinity when we start with the ideal of a Trinitarian God. If we start with Christology and make the ideal of a Trinitarian God secondary, then the other persons are just ancillary. We must reframe the way we think about blackness or everything besides identity will always be ancillary. The beauty of a Trinitarian framework is it opens our minds to other ways of expressing blackness, ways that are invitational and move us toward capturing new glimpses of what we mean by the term black.

Second, the concept of perichoresis as a way to think about how African Americans should relate to one another is helpful. Perichoresis is often referred to as the divine dance or the way the persons of the Trinity make space for one another in community. To model perichoresis is to make space intentionally for others to be black in their own way and not some idealized way. It also means working toward the flourishing of all in the community. The Trinity gives us a glimpse of all the persons in the God-head, while at the same time pointing us toward the transformation of all things that the God-head is moving toward. When theologians talk about the Trinity, a distinction is often made between the immanent and economic Trinity. The immanent Trinity is God's relationship with God's self.[64] The economic Trinity is what gets revealed to the world or the way in which God relates to the world.[65] Many theologians believe what is revealed to us in the economic Trinity is true to who God is in the immanent Trinity. In other words, what is revealed to us in the world is not an act, but true to God's nature. Because of this it is not possible to speak of the economic and immanent Trinity as two completely separate ideas.[66]

The relationship between the economic and immanent Trinity is an important model for the African American community. The importance of making space for one another and creating a dynamic and relational community will change how we dialogue publicly. We are not suggesting a retreat or some inward focus for the African American community because long-term public engagement is critical. We are suggesting, however, that the conversation on blackness can benefit from creating different internal ways of relating that will translate into a different public dialogue. The idea of making space for one another is not about valuing some voices over others. It is not about developing a single front to which everyone in the community adheres. It is about a different way of being in community that promotes healing[67] and making space for others to be a part of the conversation. This truly does require a divine dance. To be more precise a dance empowered by the Holy Spirit.[68] It is a new way of relating that is not reductionist and honors difference within the community. It is a Trinitarian way of relating.

Finally, it is important to say a few words about how a different theological perspective can alter public discourse about blackness. We began this chapter by talking about some of the ways blackness gets discussed in religion, politics, and society. The challenge is to move beyond oppositional ways of thinking about blackness. We are suggesting another theological way forward is to move to a Trinitarian model and not solely focus on Christology.

This shift reframes public discourse on blackness by moving away from oppositional ways of being toward a model that makes space for various ways of being black. The debate between Smiley and Sharpton should not focus on whether the president's agenda is black enough. We continually return to who defines the criteria for what is black enough. A different way of framing the debate is, "Where are Obama's policies making a difference for African Americans?" and "What is that difference?" These questions do not lose sight of the particularity of blackness, but shift the debate away from being strictly about identity to the welfare of African Americans.

The truth is Obama's policies[69] are probably helping some African Americans and hurting others. Simply claiming to be Malcolm X black or King black is not a way to reflect on the difference the policies are making. Gender and class have as much to do with the affect of the policies as the question of identity. The goal is to engage in an authentic conversation that holds Obama accountable as a part of the community and not categorize him as an outsider simply because he has a different perspective than some.

Obama is not the only one to be held accountable. Smiley and Sharpton are also accountable to the community. We are all part of the dance and no one gets to sit it out. An authentic conversation is not about pointing fingers, but calls us to action. This may mean going around the room and inviting those left out to the floor. It may require transporting some to the dance or moving the dance to where they are located. What is not acceptable is to place blame on another part of the community and think we are exempt.

This is an important shift and one that will challenge us to think very differently about what it means to be black. No longer is it acceptable to stake one's claim to blackness solely on identification with a particular figure or tradition. To be black is about identity and much more. We have tended to ignore the more and those seeking to construct different understandings of blackness that do not fit neatly into preconceived categories. Our belief is when we shift the way we construct the conversation within African American communities to recognize various ways of being black, it enriches the conversation. Not only will it enrich the conversation in African American communities, but it will also make the external conversation richer because more voices will be informing the dialogue. Let's stop debating about who is black and who is not. Instead, we need to hear from all voices as we continuously construct and reconstruct the meaning of blackness.

# 6

# Reclaiming the Prophetic: Toward a Theology of Hope and Justice in a Fragmented World

An idea to reclaim prophetic dimensions of biblical narratives arises from the fact that God calls us to think and act in relation to all spheres of human experience—social, political, economic, and religious. The 2008 presidential election created a hopeful perspective for many individuals (e.g., those who never imagined anyone except a Euro American male being president) toward a more holisitic integration of what it means to be human. In part, this was due to the way in which then Senator Barack Obama seemingly challenged the status quo. One could argue he prophetically challenged the status quo. As we reflect on the weeks preceding the 2012 presidential election, Peter Paris' assertion, "the king can never be prophet, nor the prophet king,"[1] prompts us to consider what it means for one who is in power to speak truth to power.

A quick perusal of the Bible illustrates Paris' point. Those called prophets in Israel were not kings, and most of the kings of Israel were not prophetic. Even David during the peak of his power, is called back in line by Nathan—prophet of Israel during that time. A challenge today is not simply seeking a prophetic voice that does not fall prey to the lure of power. Rather, a presenting dilemma is how to create an environment that is prophetic so that we are not dependent on one voice. In part, this was the power of Obama's "yes we can" chant during the 2008 presidential campaign. It was not about one person standing out. It was about all of us playing a role to make a difference.

Weeks before the 2012 presidential election, cultural problems of nihilism, capitalistic desire, and the progressive allure of technology were prime indicators that a prophetic environment may not be readily apparent. A prophetic environment is that space where all individuals, with specific concerns for individuals most adversely affected by an extended global economic crisis and decades long wars on multiple continents, can experience true humanity. Constructing a prophetic environment cannot be the work of one individual (e.g., King or Obama) it requires a prophetic response by everyone. By prophetic response, we mean an intentional call to engage in passionate and courageous action to help uplift the plight of and stand in solidarity with those most vulnerable in society today.

Almost a decade ago, Leonardo Boff, a pioneer in the development of Liberation Theology, rightly observed that "we are entering a new phase of humankind, a new level of consciousness, and a new age for the planet Earth."[2] Boff helps us to understand the importance of acting courageously in terms of the planet. These sweeping changes, he argued, will shape the ways in which Christianity and other world religions seek to "maintain and communicate a common message to all human beings and give a meaning to the universe."[3] Boff raises key questions related to the rise of what he calls the "new kind of consciousness of global proportions, a new kind of reasoning that embraces the complexities of reality and a new cosmology."[4] He asked:

1. What will happen to the two-thirds of human beings, sons and daughters of the Earth, that find themselves marginalized in this global era?[5]
2. What is the function of religions, particularly Christianity, in devising the very thing (i.e., technology, cyberspace, digital communication) that connects and reconnects all phenomena;

and that, in the religious sphere, deciphers the Sacred and the Mystery that are proclaimed within this emerging reality and that can unite and centralize all human experience?

3. What is the responsibility of each of us in bringing about deep changes that are synchronized with the wider picture of things?[6]

Boff's observations are quite compelling when we examine deeper epistemological assumptions, such as modern understandings of reason and personal autonomy, that continue to sustain oppressive systems and structures in the United States and globally. Differences related to our epistemological presuppositions affect authorities and foundations that serve to legitimate or delegitimate bodies of knowledge, which are also profoundly reflected in institutional and systemic structures. For example, the idea that Obama becoming president would instantaneously change the lives of most African Americans negates the systemic ills inherent in US culture. Differences concerning race, culture, gender, sexuality, geography, theology, and ethics often reflect competing and shared epistemological visions of the world. The world views to which we refer are those expressed in systems of patriarchy, racism, sexism, homophobia, and even larger social and political systems such as socialism, totalitarianism, capitalism, and neocolonialism, which often result in how we continue to create space for voiceless, victimized, and aliened bodies crying out to be heard.

Evidence supports that electing an African American to the highest political office in the United States is no guarantee that progress will be made when it comes to poverty, health care, the incarcerated, education, and the continuous onslaught of global war and nuclear proliferation. According to the World Health Organization (WHO), about 1.2 billion people now live in extreme poverty—living on the equivalent of less than a dollar a day[7] while millions are locked out of economic processes due to a lack of capital which is necessary in order to participate in the current global market system. What is at stake is a socially responsible market system that values human life and, at the same time, provides space for innovation and autonomy.

## Race, Politics, and Religion in a Postmodern World

Because of dramatic global disparities, it is critical to probe intersections of race, politics, and religion. The issue of race, in particular, continues to be a major subject of discussion in the public square as the United States and much of the world continues to struggle with racism and religious intolerance.[8] It is fitting to offer a brief survey of the current context of race in the United States, its connections to the global Church and public life; and what it means for us as we seek to build a constructive vision of hope, justice, and racial inclusivity and uniqueness as we move into the future.

There is a sense in which many have grown weary from talking about race, racial difference, and racism. During the 2008 and 2012 presidential campaigns, race was an unavoidable and continual subtext. Then Senator Obama's speech on race in Philadelphia on March 18, 2008, spoke directly to the issue of race and his own personal journey as a person of mixed racial ancestry. However, since assuming office, there has been very little if any sustained national discussions of race or racial differences in the nation.

Many debates and conversations around race and its connections to politics have been ongoing since the eighteenth and nineteenth centuries. Walker's Appeal, by David Walker, published September 1829, called for the radical abolishment of slavery with recognition of racial equality and inclusivity.[9] Walker, even then, was aware of the devastating implications of globalization, as the slave trade represented one of the earliest expressions of the normalization of global trade. Slavery created the conditions under which British, European, and North American markets could flourish and grow at unprecedented rates. The global scale of slavery in Brazil, the Americas, and

Caribbean supports the expansion of trade across Asia, the Middle East, and Europe.[10]

One detects this early struggle with race and difference in reading Georg Wilhelm Friedrich Hegel's *The Philosophy of History*, wherein he situated Europe and German culture as the center and crowning culmination of human civilization.[11] Hegel, along with René Descartes, Immanuel Kant, Edmund Burke, the Marquis de Condorcet and others helped give rise to what some have described as modernity or a cultural, political, and philosophical movement that "refers to the new civilization developed in Europe and North America over the last several centuries."[12] While there is much debate and disagreement over what constitutes "modernity" and its counterpart "modernism," the fact remains that this new way of life, which privileges rationalism, technological development and individual autonomy, has affected life in the United States in every dimension—art, music, literature, theology, the church, and social systems. The modern preoccupation with reason and personal autonomy, which was cast as normative for all human beings, led to much of the thinking that contributed to the advent of colonialism, slavery, free-market capitalism, pervasive "neo-colonialism," and many of the tragic side effects of globalization today. These modern presuppositions also contributed to heightened sensitivities to connections between race and power, as well as race's relationship to economics, militarism, and imperialism.

The postmodern world, which seems to be at once both modern and postmodern, is a world governed by a demand for individualism, personal autonomy, fragmentation, and both incredulity and openness to differences. It is a world that is at the same time both interconnected and fragmented. We now have access to massive amounts of information through cyberspace—that is; social networking sites like Twitter, Facebook, flicker, blogs, texting; and digital communication forms in television, radio, and transcontinental travel. It is a world in which, as Martin Luther King Jr. described it in *Where Do We Go from Here: Chaos or Community?* "a family unduly separated in ideas, culture and interest, who, because we can never again live apart, must learn somehow to live with each other in peace."[13]

In many ways, the circumstances surrounding the earthquake in Haiti on January 12, 2010, is indicative of a broader plight of the poor, disproportionately appearing in the black and brown skinned peoples of the world. Can any of us deny the frightening parallels between Hurricane Katrina of 2005 and the earthquake in Haiti? Both seemed to particularly affect the poorest, most vulnerable among us, downtrodden black folks who seem to lack essential resources to respond resolutely to their own tragedy. While New Orleanians and Haitians have sought, with pain, struggle, and dignity, to overcome atrocities of the past, both still contend with feeling the brunt of slavery's past and a generational history of systemic racism, poverty, and social and political neglect. When tragedies such as these arise, it can cause us to question profoundly the nature of our faith, understandings of God, and the way the world is ordered.

There is a sense in which the meaninglessness of the awful tragedy of the earthquake in Haiti reflects the ongoing suffering of black folks in the United States and throughout the African Diaspora. An appraisal of the African American experience today is quiet revealing. It points to a "canary in the mine" or indicator of some of the endemic societal challenges of this nation as a whole. As James Cone observed at the 2009 American Academy of Religion meeting in Montreal, Canada, there are more black people in prison or jail today than there were at the height of the civil rights movement, when mass incarceration was a common occurrence. Worldwide, the data is even more compelling.[14] Prior to the earthquake, the average Haitian was living on less than 20 cents a day. In most developing nations, primarily in Africa, Central and South America, and Asia, most people live on less than a dollar a day.

## Reclaiming the Prophetic Tradition for Our Time

Based on the above summary data, we contend there is ample cause for outrage, albeit prophetic rage. Prophetic rage is not simply an emotional or pathological response to meaning-lessness and human suffering. It is not merely an intellectual response to the social, political, and philosophical problems of modern day culture. It is a comprehensive, holistic (mind and body) perspective that draws on the collective wisdom, strength, resilience, and faith of the biblical prophetic tradition, prophetic voices throughout history, as well as the narratives of enslaved Africans who faced down the dogs of meaninglessness and suffering through a militate determination to be free, human, and dignified agents of their own existence.

The biblical prophetic tradition stands as a testimony to the ways in which people of faith have, in times past, mustered up creative resources not only to resist the tyranny of slavery, violence of the ancient world, and political oppression, but triumph in the face of untold suffering as well. They did so by first recognizing that God, as creator, comes to establish God's way of being in the world. God's way of being, the existence that God seeks to establish, is a reality that is just, good, free, and beautiful. In this tradition, they affirmed that God encounters human beings both as individual, autonomous persons and collectively as a people who exist in interconnected social groups (communities, societies, civilizations, states, even empires). Because this tradition was not beholden to the rigid, binary systems of thinking (of the Enlightenment), the questions raised and modes of social ordering had less to do with "who does what, when, how and where," but focused instead on what does it mean to live in a way that establishes God's way of being in the world.

It was this prophetic tradition that guided the history of martyrdom both in the church and among other great voices who have stood against systemic evils.[15] Throughout history, there have been those courageous individuals who have, in spite of their existential situation, resisted injustice.[16] They did so not necessarily with an awareness that full moral victory would occur in their lifetimes or that their personal or collective sacrifices would achieve its desired goals. They were able to engage in revolutionary acts because they recognized that the process of resisting injustice, establishing God's peace and justice in the world, was itself, a moral victory. The process of speaking truth to power, lifting ones voice in opposition to what is wrong, in proclamation for what is right, embodies a kind of generative, life giving force that enables individuals and groups to thrive and flourish even amid incredible odds.

Albert Raboteau, in *Slave Religion: The Invisible Institution in the Antebellum South*, discussed ways in which enslaved Africans, a deeply religious people in their own right, were able to construct sophisticated theological understandings of God as a counter-revolutionary practice for resistance and survival.[17] Richard Allen, founder of the African Methodist Episcopal Church, as well as Henry Highland Garnett, David Walker, Sojourner Truth, Phillis Wheatley, and Frederick Douglass captured the essence of the enslaved African's will to be free, to live with justice and human dignity even as the social and political context, intellectual structures and theological teachings were all designed to perpetuate black dehumanization and subjugation. According to Raboteau, many of the systems and structures in southern life during slavery, from religion to politics and cultural practices, were designed and constructed in a way that was meant to keep enslaved Africans in bondage. These systems contributed to the formation of a society fundamentally divided by racial identity, laying the ground work for what attorney Derrick Bell called the permanence of race in America. The racial divides of slavery serve as the backdrop of contemporary racial politics in the nation today, as seen in the election of the nation's first black president in 2008.[18]

What makes the 2008 presidential election and the Obama Administration such an intriguing subject of reflection is that, in many ways, Obama's life and events around his election serve as compelling illustrations of the convergence of race and politics. On the backdrop of these radical changes we now witness a rapidly changing global society. Since the late 1960s, with the rise of the information age and growth of global markets, the United States has become rapidly more diverse and multicultural. Sweeping changes concerning the racial make up of the nation have been brought into being largely because of increasing transcontinental trade, global travel, technological advances in global communication, and mass media networks as well. People from vastly different races and cultures from all around the world are now compelled to live together, work together, worship together, and occupy the same geopolitical spaces like never before in human history. These radical changes in racial and cultural differences, coupled with technology and global communication, demonstrate a need for renewed conversations on reconciliation and social justice.

Before we set the stage for a constructive theology of hope and justice in a fragmented world, there are several key contextual points that should be established:

1. The Obama presidency is as much about race as it is about politics and economics. We cannot separate the policies that now confront the nation—from health care to education, prison reform, unemployment, taxation, international policy with the war in Afghanistan—from the reality of race. Furthermore, Obama's presidency makes sense only in light of the United States' historical context as informed by its interrelated history of racism, white supremacy, and capitalism.

2. The Obama administration stands as an intricate part of the Black Freedom Struggle, and the larger global liberation movements and anticolonial struggles worldwide. It was not surprising, for instance, that Obama was awarded the Nobel Peace Prize, not for what he had accomplished, but as a hopeful boost of encouragement for what much of the world hopes his administration will accomplish, particularly in relation to the suffering of the world's poor, the devastating effect of militarism and economic exploitation, and new opportunities to address global warming.

3. All politics is local. For instance, in a city such as Louisville, Kentucky, there is a direct relationship between local issues and the rigorous political struggles in Washington, DC, and across the world. Mitch McConnell, the Senate Minority Whip from Kentucky, has been one of the most outspoken opponents of President Obama's health-care reform, even though the vast majority of citizens in Kentucky, most of whom make less than $30,000 annually, will benefit from this reform initiative. Political leaders such as McConnell are intricately involved in establishing public policies that affect millions, dramatically felt

especially in local spaces. Nuanced and coded racial sub themes continue to be one of the chief strategies used by large multinational pharmaceutical companies and the health-care industry to manipulate public opinion toward the status quo.

4. The Obama administration must be supported, challenged, and engaged at the local level by compelling locally elected leaders to respond to pressing local issues.

5. We have an opportunity, perhaps like never before in the history of our nation, to push for sweeping social change to advance a sense of equality and justice for all US residents. Only by organizing a collective response that reflects concerns of blacks, whites, Latinos, rich and poor, liberal and conservative, can we stem a rampant tide of economic and political exploitation and social neglect. According to Johnny B. Hill, we should push the Obama Administration to introduce an American Truth and Reconciliation Commission, similar to what took place in South Africa and other countries.[19] Such a commission would focus solely on unearthing varied stories of struggle, racial difference, injustice, and intolerance as it appears in multiple forms based on race, gender, sexual orientation, religion, or cultural designators.

We challenge a notion that somehow Obama's presidency marks an end to racism or the inauguration of a new, burgeoning, "postracial society."[20]

Postracial, like "color-blind society," is deeply problematic on at least two levels. It minimizes distinctive narratives, experiences, cultures, languages, and heritages of individuals and groups. We also find it deeply troubling that anyone would want to aspire toward a "postracial society." Instead, it is our premise that we should work toward a world that celebrates differences, affirms stories, cultures, and ideas among individuals irrespective of racial, ethnic, religious and/or other identities. At the same time, in our differences, we must strive toward a process by which we struggle with our unique understandings of justice and equality for all.

Closely associated with the Obama Presidency, relative to race relations, is what appears to be a tendency that advances a mythological image of black progress that frequently distorts realities of racial disparities and racial separation in the United States. On the one hand, blacks continue to thrive and overcome despite magnanimous barriers (i.e., inequities in public education, housing, the prison industrial complex, unemployment, etc.).[21] On the other hand, statistically, black Americans still lag behind in net worth and income, educational attainment, and general social well-being.[22]

## The Prophetic Task and the Black Freedom Struggle

Now, in a post-Civil Rights era, there is a critical need to reassess the nature of the 1960s civil rights movement and Martin Luther King Jr.'s legacy, in general.[23] To this end, we offer a few brief observations that may contribute to a constructive and prophetic vision for black flourishing and racial equality that have long-term implications.

If the black freedom struggle is to move ahead, we must begin to "think globally and act locally." Technological, global travel, and mass communication enhancements that occur at rapid speeds now enable people of faith and the broader public to connect synchronously with people in nearly any location in the world. This reality should cause us to reimagine our own place in the world as well as our personal and social responsibilities to help reshape communities. Our coworkers, institutions with which we are affiliated, ideas that capture our attention, and our communities of faith, are all global and multicultural in makeup. One of the greatest barriers to building a sense of collective consciousness today is the fact that black communities are more diverse than ever before. Like President Obama—who has both a white and an African parent, grew up in Hawaii and Indonesia, and was raised by and large by his white mother and her parents—the social and racial identity of black life today is deeply fragmented and fluid. We must embrace a pluralistic, diverse, and global vision of black life that is expansive and global. For instance, we must begin to see our connection with our African heritage and ancestry as a basis from which to build a common struggle. Afrocentric thinkers such as Molefi Asanti and Randal Robinson have made similar claims of a need for solidarity across the African Diaspora. They argue that a common African heritage must be the lens through which blacks approach politics, economics, and cultural life.[24]

The prophetic task before us today must focus on common values that are multidimensional in scope. Historically, since W. E. B. Du Bois published his now classic *The Souls of Black Folks* in 1903, collective consciousness and Black solidarity are critical to advancing the black plight.[25] At the turn of the twentieth century, Black leaders were reluctant to openly challenge other black leaders for fear of alienation or criticism for undermining black progress.[26] Now, we have entered a context when black politics is much more complex. For instance, Obama's presidency is a historical triumph in a country characterized, though not exclusively, by a history of slavery, racism, and Jim Crow segregation. In light of this, blacks as well as whites had much cause to celebrate Obama's first term and possibilities that his reelection might yield.

However, when Obama stood on January 20, 2009, to take the oath of office to protect and defend The Constitution of the United States from enemies foreign and domestic, he became intertwined with principalities and powers that govern the entrenched political systems in this nation. Whatever prophetic mantle (or sense of vocational identity as one who calls the nation to some higher moral vision) may have been on Barack Obama during his 2008 presidential campaign and his tenure as a community organizer became replaced with the biblical role as "king" or the one who governs. Central to a prophetic task is an individual and communal commitment to continue to work toward establishing God's ways of being in the world. In addition, a prophetic dictate also requires that we think and act with a generational consciousness. To think and act with a generational consciousness means to live with an awareness that present circumstances are rooted in a history steeped in struggle and resilience. That we as human beings live as agents of historical contingencies, and yet we have an opportunity to shape that history even as it is coming into being. The promise of every new emerging generation brings with it the hope of a brighter day.

German philosopher and poet Johann Wolfgang von Goethe once observed that the "destiny of any nation rests in the hands of its young people."[27] We must move swiftly, therefore, with prophetic urgency, to cultivate leaders for present and future generations. Currently, there is not only a crisis of leadership in the black community[28] but a crisis of black intellectualism, which in recent years has grossly neglected the task of black leadership. Part of this is accounted for by class divides in black communities. As Mary Pattillo pointed out in *Black on the Block: The Politics of Race and Class in the City*, there are deep wedges along class lines in the black community, marked by educational attainment and income.[29] It appears most acutely in terms of residential segregation and educational institutions. This challenge is related to the structural nature of higher education, which still leans toward a Eurocentric privileged system that favors a ruling class orientation.[30] Eboo Patel's Interfaith Youth Core is an example of the kinds of innovative ideas geared toward building an inclusive, dynamic, and progressive global vision of community and peace that involves young people.[31]

The black community, the church, and US society as a whole must confront the ravishing nature of our current culture of consumption and materialism as well as justice issues that create new forms of pseudo slavery. Elements of pseudo slavery are seen in the reality of grossly underfunded, predominately black public schools across the country and the related prison industrial complex. In *The New Jim Crow: Mass Incarceration in the Age of Colorblindness*, Michelle Alexander observed that social conditions such as inequities in public education, housing, unemployment, and health care have contributed to the making of a new form of legalized discrimination, especially among poor blacks.[32] The draconian nature of the current judicial system has produced a permanent underclass, largely labeled as "criminal," stripped of citizen's rights and exhibiting many of the same characteristics of a slave class. Alexander argued that the cradle to prison pipeline in many poor black communities is not accidental but has become a chief means of social control, similar to slavery and segregation in the mid-twentieth century. These realities, she wrote, cannot be divorced from a culture of consumption that informs black aspirations and markers of achievement and success.[33]

The Black community and its leaders (that include black politicians, intellectuals, church leaders, and entrepreneurs) must begin to think critically about the ways in which we participate in our own oppression through involvement in a culture of materialism and unending consumption. Likewise, we must challenge economic disparities that continue to plague poor communities in this country and abroad. This involves tracing economic connections linked to mass incarceration, unemployment, housing, and public education. We must forge creative connections and relationships with diverse racial ethnic groups in order to advance communities of justice, peace, freedom, and equality for all.

## Toward a Theology of Hope and Justice Today

Ultimately, challenges that confront oppressed peoples, particularly the poor, serve as a contextual perspective to build a constructive and prophetic theology of hope and justice. Although various theologies of liberation have experienced extensive criticisms in recent years for Marxist overtones and appeals to social theory, it has nevertheless served as an important reminder of the need to listen to voices on life's margins, in the shadows, and at the periphery to understand what justice means.[34] A fundamental task of the Church is to live out God's vision of peace, justice, and community.

At the center of this question is the language of justice and exactly what constitutes justice. Aquinas offers a helpful distinction regarding justice. For Aquinas there are two kinds of justice—commutative justice and distributive justice. Commutative justice refers to the direct exchange of goods and services. It applies to the temporal and material reality of daily existence. Commutative justice is isolated solely to the process of buying and selling. Distributive justice relates to the equal distribution of resources consistent with the being itself. Aquinas argues that

God's justice may be seen as distributive since God defines what justice is and because it is consistent with God's nature.[35]

Allow us to suggest that in order to address challenges ascribed to nihilism and fragmentation that so pervade postmodern consciousness, the church must look to a pre-Constantinian Christian faith community that attempted to live in a radical and peculiar fashion. It is a community that took seriously the social, economic, political, and cultural dynamics of faith. Only when allegiances to Christ became interwoven with allegiances to the state did believers begin to surrender the prophetic zeal of what it means to live in Christian community.[36] Attempting to reconcile citizenship in the kingdom of God and the state created the kind of split loyalties and conflicts that have plagued faithful Christian witnesses throughout history.

Here, to recover a sense of the "prophetic" means to address epistemological underpinnings of modern culture. In short, we must begin to address not only what we do and think in the West but also how and why we do what we do. The footprints of figures like Martin Luther King Jr., Nelson Mandela, Desmond Tutu, Mother Teresa, Mahatma Gandhi, and Oscar Romero give us clues not only as examples of faithful Christian witness but also on how to do theology today. These individuals present a method that responds to the pluralistic postmodern distrust of totalizing theological or religious systems that claims hegemonic privileges over all others. These figures present a pragmatic theological approach where God-talk is given currency by the ways in which it speaks to the suffering and hope of the downtrodden and oppressed.

The aforementioned persons challenge Cartesian and Hegelian models of philosophical and theological discourse, which has embedded in its language a hegemonic bias toward the way rationalism is defined and constructed. When, in the fourteenth century, Decartes proclaimed that personal autonomy and individual reason are the marks of what it means to be human, he denied the inherent social nature of human life.[37] Advancing this idea, Hegel crowned German culture, and the West more generally, as the culmination of human rational achievement, casting the African and Oriental worlds as subordinate in moral and intellectual capacities. Reading Hegel's Philosophy of History closely gives insights to the foundational systems at work in theology emerging from the nineteenth century and throughout the twentieth century.[38]

Within African American religious experiences, there are several key figures and documents that may hold clues to faithful prophetic Christian witness today. Henry Highland Garnett, Sojourner Truth, Frederick Douglass, the various Kairos Documents throughout the world, and Martin Luther King Jr.'s *Letter from Birmingham Jail* are among the many voices and documents that reflect the demand for God's radical call to justice and hope in every generation and society.[39] Within the last 20 years, several Kairos documents have emerged as a prophetic call for the church to respond to social and structural realities that affect those bodies pushed out of the centers of political and economic power (i.e., underrepresented groups whose interests are often not addressed in the prevailing social, political, and economic structures in that context). The first of these was the Kairos Document: Challenge to the Church, which appeared in South Africa in 1985. The Kairos Central America appeared in 1988, and The Road to Damascus: Kairos and Conversion was developed in 1989, a collaborative effort of South African, Asian, and Central American origins.[40] An earlier example of documents similar to Kairos, was a status confessionis, a response of the Confessing Church in Germany where it essentially declared that supporting Hitler was in direct contradiction to what it means to be Christian. Articulated in the Barmen Declaration, issued in May 1934, the document was primarily written by the Swiss theologian, Karl Barth.[41]

The following words from the South African Kairos document depict the urgent nature to understand the historical situation that compels believers toward action. It reads:

> Kairos is the Greek word that is used in the Bible to designate a special moment of time when God visits [God's] people to offer them a unique opportunity for repentance and conversion, for change and decisive action. It is a time of judgment. It is a moment of truth, a crisis.[42]

These sentiments, further illuminated in the Kairos Central America document, reveal that:

> Central America has become a Kairos of unforeseeable consequences: either we close the door on the possibility of hope for the poor for many years, or as prophets we open up a new Day for humanity and thus for the Church.[43]

For many, God is a God of the poor who seeks to liberate them from not only the moral and spiritual elements that restrict their ways of being, but also from systematic forces that inform their life of faith.

The Asian theological document Road to Damascus poignantly attends to the critical nature of elevating the condition of the poor and persecuted to the center in its assertion that:

> God is on the side of the poor, the oppressed, the persecuted. When this faith is proclaimed and lived in a situation of political conflict between the rich and the poor, when the rich and the powerful reject this faith and condemn it as heresy, we can read the signs and discern something more than a crisis. We are faced with a Kairos, a moment of truth, a time for decision, a time of grace, a God-given opportunity for conversion and hope.[44]

Here, the writers reflect on the biblical account of Saul on the Damascus Road where he is confronted with the reality of two competing theological visions. He is faced with either the God of the religious and political authorities who killed a first-century Palestinian Jewish agitator and extremist or the God who sides with the One crucified as a blasphemer.[45] In either case, the tension of a kairos moment (or moment of decision) points to theological commitments at stake that either liberate, or sustain, the poor and dispossesseds' suffering.

Historically, many liberation theologians have tended to focus on the crucifixion as the meeting place of divine concern and human suffering. James Cone's *A Black Theology of Liberation* and Gustavo Gutierrez's *Liberation Theology* both pave the way as key texts that *examine* human suffering through the lens of the crucifixion.[46] Cone and Gutierrez, along with scholars like Jacquelyn Grant, Katie Geneva Cannon, Delores Williams, Rosemary Ruether, Letty Russell, Leonardo Boff, and others view the cross as a symbol of divine companionship in human pain and suffering. The cross has come to represent, for those who suffer, the God who reveals God's-self as the one who suffers with the feeble, broken, and disquieted bodies of marginalized and oppressed peoples. God's reconciling activity does not come through power, dominance, and coercive influence. Rather, God's reconciling activity comes through humility, persuasion, and meekness. Christ's sufferings, therefore, are recognized as a form of vindication and divine companionship for the abandoned, abused, neglected, and exploited. Particularly within the frameworks of Latin American liberation theologies and black theologies of liberation, the cross has become a lens through which to understand how God champions the cause of liberation and hope in the world. The cross reveals whom God ultimately stands with and how God chooses to reconcile God's world.

## Hope: A Contextual Understanding

Justice gives rise to hope. Justice motivates and inspires hope. Perhaps injustice is the great threat to hope. Hope suggests that the story (or historical narrative of freedom, justice, and equality) is untold, that there is more to the story. Narrative theology and the storytelling tradition of many indigenous cultures around the world are helpful resources to advance conversations related to justice. Additionally, to build a constructive theology of justice also means to think about a contextually based theology of hope. In the Christian tradition, hope has been historically located in the area of the eschatological vision of God's ultimate redemption and transformation of the world.[47] The mid-century theologies of hope inspired by German theologian Jürgen Moltmann and Latin American liberation theologian Gustavo Gutierrez is useful in today's fragmented world inasmuch as they give specificity to what the fulfillment of the Kingdom of God means for the oppressed.

J. Deotis Roberts, reflecting on the black experience in the United States, provides, for instance, a graphic and illustrative summary. Roberts reminds us that "Heaven as a reward at some unforeseeable future time brings little hope to the hungry and mistreated black person. Hell-future makes little impression upon blacks living in hell-present of shacks, rats, roaches, hunger, unemployment, and inhuman treatment."[48] Roberts' account of hope, though constrained within the perimeters of black experience, may also be useful as one way to understand the meaning of hope for other oppressed groups as well. Serious reflection on what God is doing to make life more humane in the present is a basis to comprehend more fully what God intends to do in the age to come.

Within a Christian African American religious tradition, the resurrection has often been viewed as a declaration of divine judgment. It is, in other words, redemption from unwarranted and meaningless historical exploitation and abuse. For instance, when Martin Luther King Jr., days after the initiation of the Montgomery Bus boycott, stood on his ruined doorsteps after a bombing and told the concerned who gathered to inquire about his family's safety that "unmerited and unprovoked suffering can have meaning in the quest for freedom and justice," his prophetic utterance and consistent insistence on a nonviolent response signaled that an ability to deal with current realities of suffering comes from a faithful affirmation informed by possibilities that are intricately connected to the resurrection event.

## Reconciliation

A constructive task to develop meaningful theologies of justice and hope within today's world must be grounded in commitment to a process of reconciliation. Justice and hope as coagulate themes do not stand outside of reconciliation but remain at the center of tasks and end-goals. The classical doctrine of reconciliation has emphasized justification and sanctification as central themes.[49] The classical doctrine of reconciliation does little in the way of challenging structures that perpetuate systems of oppression. Nevertheless, there is a critical need to explore the contours of the doctrine of sanctification because it attends to human agency. As depicted in the reading, "God was in Christ reconciling the world unto God's self" thus giving Christians a ministry of reconciliation. The central concern, then, is not what God has done in Christ, but rather how believers live more faithfully into their calling as agents of reconciliation.

The prophetic call is a teleological declaration of reconciliation. It is reconciliation with liberation since there can only be reconciliation among equals when the dignity and personhood of individuals are recognized and celebrated through community and otherness. African and African American perspectives have much to teach the world when it comes to reconciliation. In spite of centuries of violent oppression and hostility, African peoples have, by in large, responded nonviolently and with an expressed commitment to forgiveness and restorative justice.

Specifically, the work of reconciliation in South Africa is an important example of ways in which reconciliation functions as a method of social, political, and economic transformation. Admittedly, there are still a great many problems that plague South Africans in a postapartheid environment. In fact, land ownership, economic disparities, and a series of health-related concerns remain top priorities for church and state. At the same time, the majority black South African populations now have an opportunity to participate, through a purported democratic process, in their own future and destiny as a people. Tutu's ubuntu theology challenged Western notions of rationalism and autonomy, affirming that human fulfillment is achieved in relationship with others.[50] In the aftermath of South African apartheid, Tutu observed that there is something about deep suffering and hurt that brings about compassion, sympathy, and the power of forgiveness.[51] What was unique about the South African experience was the intentionality given to story-telling as a method to expose wounds of the past in order to build a more hopeful and equitable future.

Local and global conflicts near and far seem to be intensifying like never before in human history. If we are to stem a tide of violence and global conflict, reconciliation, with justice and hope, must become a central mission of the Church and public life in the United States of America and around the world. Truly, now is the time to act swiftly, boldly, passionately, and prophetically for the cause of hope, justice, and reconciliation in our local communities and distant lands. King's words are a fitting conclusion to our discussion. As he observed, "we are now faced with the fact that tomorrow is today...We are confronted with the fierce urgency of now. In this unfolding conundrum of life and history there is such a thing as being too late. Procrastination is a thief of time. Life often leaves us standing bare, naked and dejected with a lost opportunity."[52] Similarly, Mother Teresa of Calcutta simplistically proclaimed: "Unless a life is lived for others, it is not worthwhile." And, "God doesn't require us to succeed; he [God] only requires that we try."[53]

# 7

# The World House: The Beloved Community as a New Global Vision for Peace and Justice

Many people still revel in the January 2009 historic inauguration of President Barack Hussein Obama where millions of Americans across racial, ethnic, economic, and generational lines, from every region of the world, gathered in tribute and celebration. In the shadows of rulers and leaders from distant lands and icons of the black freedom struggle like John Lewis and Joseph Lowery, it is difficult to imagine that just a generation ago the United States was on the brink of catastrophe as the country struggled emotionally to respond to the assassination of Martin Luther King Jr. on April 4, 1968, in Memphis, Tennessee—which produced shockwaves that reverberated around the globe. It has, perhaps, not been since that dramatic gathering of Americans in the Selma campaign of 1965–1966 that such a massive multicultural, multireligious, and multiracial coalition was assembled in terms of what was achieved during the 2008 presidential election. As the first year of President Obama's second term draws to a close, it is truly an opportune time to reflect critically and imaginatively on the legacy of Martin Luther King Jr. and his creative vision of the beloved community. From this point of departure, we will reflect on the way in which King's legacy of the beloved community offers a constructive theological and ethical perspective on developing an inclusive vision of justice and reconciliation within today's context.

Regardless of one's political orientation, the 2008 presidential campaign was a magnificent display of human creativity, community, and progressive political action at work, perhaps the greatest seen in the last 40 years of the United States' democratic history. We agree with Tom Brokaw's observation that the election simply does not make sense apart from the black freedom struggle of the civil rights movement and King's prophetic vision of racial equality.

Understanding King's involvement in the civil rights movement, especially those latter years after 1963 and the crucible of Birmingham, tells us a great deal about the current social, political, and economic landscape of postmodern society as well as a need to think critically about questions of difference and otherness in a way that affirms human freedom and dignity.

The world is rapidly changing. Now more than ever before, people from all around the world (of different races, religions, cultures, class, sexual orientation, and ethnicities) are being brought into close contact. The forces of mass media, cyberspace, global economics, and transportation are intensifying the manner in which individuals are challenged to interact and coexist with differences. The reality of confronting difference inevitably brings with it questions of how to order social life together, which is deeply related to establishing just relationships among equals; challenging power-relations that dehumanize others on the basis of difference. An important element of thinking about the problem of difference and moving toward an expansive view of justice as a basis of social relations means, as King observed, recognizing our sense of global interrelatedness which often finds dramatic expression in our more localized interpersonal relations. It was in the Birmingham experience that King began to have a growing awareness of human interrelatedness, brought about primarily through modern technology and ingenuity, but also experienced in the global and local quest for freedom, justice, and human dignity. Taylor Branch, American historian and author of the trilogy on America during the King years, eloquently observed:

The miracle of Birmingham might have stood alone as the culmination of a freedom movement grown slowly out of Southern black churches. Yet it was merely the strongest of many tides that crested in the movement's peak years, 1963–65. They challenged, inspired, and confounded America over the meaning of simple words: dignity, equal votes, equal souls. They gripped Malcolm X along with President Johnson, buffeted the watchwords "integration" and "nonviolence," broke bodies and spirits, enlarged freedom.[1]

After King received the Nobel Peace Prize in 1964 for his leadership in the civil rights movement, King's thinking and attitude seemed to change and expand toward a more global consciousness. The epicenter of his work, as he understood it, would still be the American South, but he sought also to move further to take on issues of poverty, solidify voting rights among poor communities, and pursue a growing urge to critique the Vietnam War. He started piecing together the curious matrix of American foreign power and its relationship to racism and economics worldwide. As the day of his assassination drew closer, with prophetic precision, King seemed to anticipate, as he penned the final chapter of his last, and perhaps most critical book, *Where Do We Go from Here: Chaos or Community?*, the evolving cultural trends in technology, mass communication, and escalating militarism.[2]

In his concluding chapter, "The World House," considered to be what Robert Michael Franklin described as King's last will and testament, King outlines the urgent need for the United States and the world to move aggressively toward the "promise land of racial justice."[3] During this period, King was undergoing a dramatic stage of self-awareness and intellectual awakening as he became more aware of the sense of interrelatedness of all life and reality. As he passionately exclaimed in his *Letter from Birmingham Jail*:

> I am cognizant of the interrelatedness of all communities and states. I cannot sit idly by in Atlanta and not be concerned about what happens in Birmingham. Injustice anywhere is a threat to justice everywhere. We are caught in an inescapable network of mutuality, tied in a single garment of destiny. Whatever affects one directly affects all indirectly.[4]

In writing this letter, King gave voice to what some have described as the postmodern dilemma or the problem of meaning itself in modern life.

King understood that people around the world were beginning to call into question the very presuppositions and epistemologies that have so dominated modern life since the Enlightenment. For instance, in his Riverside Church speech, entitled "A Time to Break the Silence," King talked about the need for US policy makers to honor the cultural, religious, and political context of the Vietnamese people. He also argued in more broad terms that the United States could no longer superimpose its will and policies on foreign nations, especially through the use of violence. The struggle against segregation was profoundly connected to the anticolonial struggles across the developing world and growth of militarism to expand and stabilize foreign markets. Drawing on dialectical theology and the crisis theology movement of the early twentieth century, as well as Boston Personalism, King surmised that rationalism and personal autonomy, as hallmarks of the Enlightenment, helped perpetuate the kind of thinking that justified the system of segregation and colonialism. It made normative what Jürgen Moltmann called the "possessive individualism of modern society"[5] where consumption and ownership of both self and property defined what it meant to be human and exist as a social being. King looked to the idea of the "love-ethic of Jesus" as a way of challenging the very presuppositions and foundations of modern notions of rationalism and personal autonomy by asserting that thought and praxis were deeply intertwined. The love-ethic of Jesus was centered on the idea that the divinity of Jesus emerged from his capacity to express radical altruism toward neighbor through peaceful means. In his imaginative and courageous pilgrimage of protest, he maintained that the essence of what it means to be human involves giving one's life over to the other; that human fulfillment is measured in the capacity to serve the other. He espoused a kind of social ontology similar to the nineteenth-century political philosopher T. H. Green who argued that human beings, above all, are social beings. It is, after all, our social relations with others, according to Green, that makes each of us human. In fact, it is our capacity and need for relationships that makes human rationalism and individual autonomy intelligible.

By emphasizing the idea of the love-ethic of Jesus, King introduced a perspective on human life, and subsequently the way social systems should be ordered, that thrust him in the midst of an ongoing campaign for racial equality, political freedom, and, increasingly, economic justice. The "love-ethic of Jesus" epitomized what it means to live in community and to exist in a cooperative relationship with God. King viewed the salvific work of God in Christ ultimately as working to bring about a harmonious human community. King grounded his theology in Christian practices such as forgiveness, communal worship, giving, nonviolence, and the quest for freedom. King believed these practices stood at the center of the Christian narrative and could serve as a powerful weapon against systemic evils like segregation in the South. He was committed to the idea that the God who moves and directs history also operates in the human community to liberate the hearts, minds, and souls of those who suffer. Although King recognized the importance of being personally reconciled with God, he maintained that this reconciliation was made intelligible and meaningful in the quest for freedom and justice. It was not simply an existential pragmatic conception of freedom and justice drawn from the wells of such thinkers as Locke, Rousseau, Kant, Hegel, Bacon, Nietzsche, Hume, and others. Rather, King planted his ideas of justice, freedom, and community firmly in the soils of a biblical prophetic tradition and an African American religious experience in the black church. His ideas were further expanded, clarified, and deepened in the rich chambers of theological reflection during his formal studies and even amid fires of protest.

There has always been a connection between theology and politics as made visible in the work of King. But as Joerg Rieger, a contemporary theologian and activist, pointed out, "the problem here is not primarily with the relation of politics and religion but with what kind of politics is supported by religion, and whether the politics of the Christian God supports the politics of empire."[6] The problem of theology, and even the church, being coopted by Empire has been present throughout history. The earliest example was the rise of Constantinianism in the fourth century, surfacing again and again in dramatic ways through colonialism from the fourteenth through the nineteenth century. Apartheid in South Africa, segregation in the United States, and political repression in Latin America as part of the legacy of the colonial era, are merely some of the examples of the cooptation of theology at the service of Empire. It has often represented a deep and persistent struggle for the church to be faithful in the face of incredible social and political injustices, such as apartheid and segregation. Michael Hardt and Antonio Negri, in *Empire*, observe that "in contrast to imperialism, Empire establishes no territorial center of power and does not rely on fixed boundaries or barriers. It is a decentered and deterritorializing apparatus of rule that progressively incorporates the entire global realm within its open, expanding frontiers."[7] Consider, as Kwok Pui-lan opined, this insightful perspective on what Empire looks like today:

> With the decline of colonial regimes since World War II and the increasingly global reach of the neo-liberal market economy, the nation-state is not as significant as before. The new Empire is defined more by economic power, secured and bolstered by military might; war becomes a continuation of politics by other means.[8]

The United States, like South Africa, with its intrinsic claims of manifest destiny, modernization, and capitalistic desire, has embodied imperial visions of the world—with apartheid and Jim Crow in their shadows.

In general, language is essential to constructing new spaces of shared meaning, peaceful coexistence, and community. Language informs culture. Language provides a free exchange of ideas, narratives, beliefs, concepts, emotions, fears, hopes, and dreams. Language has a sort of timeless character. But language is not without its limitations. Language requires interpretation and functions within a particular social, historical, and cultural medium. The language or languages we use reflects the particularity of our own history, culture, experiences, social interactions, and geopolitical context. Too often, there is an assumed universality to the language used, which reinforces the reality of its limitations. As some critics of modernity have pointed out, there is, indeed, a "gap" between language and meaning—between the symbols we use to construct language (written or spoken, verbal/nonverbal) and the meaning we attach to those symbols. Some of the critics include Gianni Vattimo in his book *The End of Modernity*, Jean Francois Lyotard's *Report on Knowledge*, and Cornel West in *Prophesy Deliverance!: An Afro-American Revolutionary Christianity.*

What is compelling about the thought and witness of King is that he offers us a way to understand the languages of peace, how it is worked out within particular historical and social circumstances, while avoiding a kind of universality that could be appropriated for all peoples, in all places, at all times. Languages of peace are the various ways in which individuals and peoples from different cultures and religious traditions have helped to advance freedom, equality, and human dignity through nonviolent means. Martin Luther King Jr., Nelson Mandela, Desmond Tutu, Mother Teresa, Dorothy Day, and Mohandas K. Gandhi came out of very different cultural, religious, and historical contexts but arrived at some of the same ideas around peace and justice. They may have spoken different languages, but communicated a shared message of peace and liberation of the oppressed. In particular, King's vision of community expresses the assertion that ultimately the language of peace and the practice of peace are part of the same reality. King's leadership in the movement challenged certain modern theological and philosophical assumptions about human nature and its implications on social and political structures throughout society. He challenged binary linguistic systems, represented by an either/or way of thinking rooted in Aristotelian and Platonic logic, that often lead to rigid distinctions and categorizations, particularly when it comes to thinking and living peace all at once.

The violence of Jim Crow segregation like apartheid in South Africa, as racialized systems of social ordering, was harmful on multiple levels. Violence was not only used as a means to sustain and maintain social control, but celebrated as a nationalistic idol for identity and meaning. The world of segregation made little sense without violence. In fact, violence gave these realities meaning. Both the threat and practice of violence were religious forces of themselves that permeated the very air of US culture. For instance, the Ku Klux Klan used violence (hangings and cross burnings) and the threat of violence, but maintained it was a Christian organization, inasmuch as many whites believed that God had ordained segregation in the United States and the execution of violence as a way to sustain a way of life.

Whether in the form of lynching, rape, denial of resources in education, medical care, and public transportation, or white supremacist ideologies, violence was fierce and insatiable. The idea of establishing separate social systems built on violence often reinforces certain modern theological and philosophical conceptions of what it means to be human. The most violent dimensions of these systems were, indeed, not just the physical violence, but psychological violence that made blacks in the south and South Africa question their dignity and personhood as God's creation. It reinforced certain pervasive messages about black life. The denial of black subjectivity or the negation of blackness in modernity felt throughout the African diaspora provides a perspective of modernity from below. The radical affirmation of subjectivity and protest during the civil rights movement and resistance against the apartheid regime were embodied critics of the linguistic, cultural, and philosophical forces of modernity in as much as modernity had characterized human life based on a particular display of rational capacities.

Most of us are familiar with the famous Cartesian saying "Cogito, ergo sum" (I think therefore I am) or "Dubito, ergo cogito, ergo sum" (I doubt, therefore I think, therefore I am). If being human means being a rational, morally conscious agent, as Cartesian and Kantian thought would have it, then there is ample cause not only to enslave but to continue to justify, even demand, demeaning treatment in order to perpetuate systems of injustice, fear, and violence. Cornel West's essay "Genealogy of Race and Modernity" in his book *Prophesy Deliverance!: An Afro American Revolutionary Christianity* is, in our opinion, the best assessment of race and modernity to date. In the essay, West traces the historical, cultural, and philosophical idea of race as an Enlightenment construct. He argues that the "binary linguistic system" of Western intellectual discourse (based on an either/or way of thinking) produced distinctions and categorizations (up/down, good/bad, right/wrong, justice/injustice, and black/white), where whiteness was equated with beauty and good, and black as its negation. These distinctions ultimately translated into a vision of social ordering based on racial and ethnic distinctions, such as those seen in Jim Crow segregation, apartheid, and colonialism.

## King, the Beloved Community, and Modernity

When King reluctantly mounted the pulpit of Holt Street Baptist Church to accept leadership of the Montgomery Improvement Association on December 5, 1955, he was not only leading an assault on the nearly one-hundred-year-old system of segregation, he, along with other freedom fighters like Ralph Abernathy, Rosa Parks, and E. D. Nixon also challenged the very foundations of modernity and the underside of American history and her dreams. King, along with other critics of modernity, such as Michel Foucault, Henry David Thoreau, Frederick Douglass, Sojourner Truth, Martin Delaney, Henry Highland Garnett, Dorothy Day, Mohandas K. Gandhi, Mother Teresa, and others, brought into question, in dramatic ways, the cultural violence of racial, economic, and political exploitation. As Charles Marsh observes in *The Beloved Community: How Faith Shapes Social Justice, from the Civil Rights Movement to Today*, King, in his address at Holt Street, situated himself within a historical and theological transformation that would have lasting implications for Montgomery and the world. Marsh wrote:

> The beautiful chaos that America would see daily on the streets of Montgomery—the tens of thousands of African Americans walking beneath a winter sky, the empty buses rolling through the capital city, the mass meetings overflowing the black churches—bear evidence of God's presence and promise. In the

passages that evoke a host of powerful biblical images—the disinherited of the land, the long night of captivity, the glimmering promise of deliverance, each image as alive with meaning for the sufferings and hopes of African Americans as it had been for Israel in the long years of exile—King describes the moment as the beginning of a larger and complicated theological drama.

King's conception of God is pragmatic in orientation, yet ontological in substance and scope.

## King's Conception of God

At the center of King's view of God was the idea that human persons are "co-workers" with God in a quest for liberation and community. Like James Cone and other liberationist theologians such as Gustavo Gutierrez, Jon Sobrino, Rosemary Ruether, Katie Geneva Cannon, Jacquelyn Grant, Delores Williams, and Ada Maria Isasi-Diaz, King believed God was on the side of those who suffer. King's God was a God of liberation and reconciliation. King drew heavily on the liberating themes of the Old Testament Exodus paradigm and the prophets to advance his understanding of justice, human freedom, and liberation.[9] However, it was the "love-ethic" of Jesus and the vision of community reflected in the Sermon on the Mount that King used to develop his understanding of community and fellowship. For King, God was not some transcendent, holy other entity detached from the harsh realities of human suffering. King resolved that the nature of God is revealed and made intelligible in a quest for social transformation and community. God revealed God's self in the redemption, healing, and restoration of the outcast and marginalized. King's God spoke to the personal needs and concerns of those who suffer. Theologian and author of *King among the Theologians*, Noel L. Erskine observed, King would reject the God of Tillich as "impersonal" and "wholly other."[10] In his dissertation at Boston University, entitled, "A Comparison of the Conceptions of God in the Thinking of Paul Tillich and Henry Nelson Wieman," King critiques Tillich's God as overly ontological.[11] Instead, King embraced personal dimensions of God as a redeemer, who relates to persons in intimate and familial ways. King's God could be expressed in the familiar refrain he often called forth, "God is a mother to the motherless, and a father to the fatherless."[12]

King's belief that humans are "co-workers" with God in social transformation is connected to his understanding of God as Redeemer. King understood God as an all-powerful creative force that redeems individuals, social systems, and institutions. As the God who redeems, God has chosen to use human persons as agents of God's transformative power in the world. Inasmuch as it is through practices, expressing the love-ethic of Jesus Christ, that the nature of God is revealed.

## Beloved Community and the Quest for Economic Justice

With a focus on holding thought and praxis in tension, King began to aggressively shift his attention from civil rights and voting rights to the broader question of human rights and poverty. He began to realize with dangerous precision that poverty stood as one of the greatest obstacles to realizing the beloved community. In 1964, King published his first proposal calling for a "Bill of Rights for the Disadvantaged." Racism, he said, was a tenacious evil, but not immutable. He saw something happening on the horizon among both poor whites and poor blacks in the south and across the country. As he wrote, "White supremacy can feed their egos but not their stomachs. They will not go hungry or forego the affluent society to remain racially ascendant."[13] He also declared:

> The curse of poverty has no justification in our age. It is socially as cruel and blind as the practice of cannibalism at the dawn of civilization, when men ate each other because they had not yet learned to take food from the soil or to consume the abundant animal life around them. The time has come for us to civilize ourselves by the total, direct and immediate abolition of poverty.[14]

After King won the Nobel Peace Prize in November 1964, he began to explore northern cities like Chicago, New York, Boston, Detroit, Cleveland, and Philadelphia. After some success with confronting and devising strategies to remedy Southern segregation, King began to recognize that the problem of poverty was intricately connected to the issue of segregation and racism in the United States. Blacks in the north found little comfort in King's vision of integration when measured against the stagnating and painful reality of ghetto life in northern cities. With the words of his acceptance speech still lingering in his mind, King said:

> I have the audacity to believe that peoples everywhere can have three meals a day for their bodies, education and culture for their minds, and dignity, equality and freedom for their spirits. I believe that what self centered men have torn down men other-centered can build up. I still believe that one day mankind will bow before the altars of God and be crowned triumphant over war and bloodshed, and nonviolent redemptive good will will proclaim the rule of the land.[15]

In Chicago, he met up with two prominent civil rights leaders, Al Raby and Meyer Weinberg, who had formed the new Coordinating Council of Community Organizations (CCCO) in order to address the problem of school integration and segregated housing.[16] It was an organizing group founded to help create the space for grievances to take place and be heard. At the same time, King was questioned consistently about his position on the Vietnam War, even as many of his Southern Christian Leadership Conference colleagues, like Benjamin Hooks, cautioned him against intervening in international affairs. Only days after the historic passage of the 1965 Voting Rights Bill on August 6, still in the shadow of the smoke filled streets of the riots in the Watts section of Los Angeles, King saw that the underlying problems of urban unrest was directly associated with increasing poverty and urbanization in Northern cities.[17] While in Chicago in 1966, King, granting a rare interview to John Herbers of the New York Times, identified two major challenges to the civil rights movement. First, he realized that the struggle to dismantle segregation was really about a much broader question of "genuine equality" to claim political and economic power for blacks. In addition, he stated that the civil rights movement was ultimately about the dignity and worth of all humans. It was this belief, King noted, that compelled him to stand up against the war in Vietnam. He came to see a deeper realization of the "interrelatedness of racism and militarism. Hence, for King, the use of international violence was as immoral for humanity as the system of racial segregation.[18]

King used the metaphor of a great "world house" to describe challenges associated with realizing the beloved community. The idea of the "world house" referred to the ways in which human beings inhabit an increasingly intimate global world. He surmised that the world did not seem as large as it once did. He understood that global and local realities were converging as a result of massive technological advances in travel, communication, and economic globalization. For King, the new situation confronting humanity was like a deeply divided family who inherited a house and must now learn to live together.

> We have inherited a large house, a great "world house" in which we have to live together—black and white, Easterner and Westerner, Gentile and Jew, Catholic and Protestant, Moslem and Hindu—a family unduly separated in ideas, culture and interest, who, because we can never again live apart, must learn somehow to live with each other in peace.[19]

He went on to say:

> All inhabitants of the globe are now neighbors. This worldwide neighborhood has been brought into being largely as a result of the modern scientific and technological revolutions. The world of today is vastly different from the world of just one hundred years ago.[20]

King was able to anticipate many of the rapidly changing realities and challenges we now see today. For example, social media enables us to connect and live in the same house in ways most of us never imagined.

Leonardo Boff described this change as synonymous to the great cultural leaps of the Iron Age and Bronze Ages of the past, when human civilizations embark upon such grand leaps that it forever changes the direction and destiny of human life. Boff and King would agree that the idea of sharing a house is not the goal of everyone in the world. King experienced this first-hand from multiple sectors. Under more and more pressure, whether from the Southern Christian Leadership Conference (SCLC) or the Federal Bureau of Investigation's increased COUNTERTEL strategies under the direction of J. Edgar Hoover to dismantle strides toward a more just society, King battled chronic depression. As he pondered both internal and external pressures, King wrote:

> One of the great liabilities of history is that all too many people fail to remain awake through great periods of social change. Every society has its protectors of the status quo and its fraternities of the indifferent who are notorious for sleeping through revolutions. But today our very survival depends on our ability to stay awake, to adjust to new ideas, to remain vigilant and to face the challenge of change. The large house in which we live demands that we transform this worldwide neighborhood into a world-wide brotherhood. Together we must learn to live as brothers or together we will be forced to perish as fools.[21]

Martin Luther King Jr. also observed that racism is not simply an American phenomenon. "It's [racism's] vicious grasp knows no geographical boundaries. In fact, racism and its perennial ally—economic exploitation—provide the key to understanding most of the international complications of this generation."[22] Many of the ongoing problems facing developing nations seem to reflect King's prophetic assertions. Even in King's time, there was a growing anti-American sentiment all across the developing world.[23] As the global economy shifted from industrial based societies to more informational based societies in the West, developing nations were the hardest hit by radical changes in global trade.[24] King called for an end to global poverty, calling it a "monstrous octopus that stretches its choking, prehensile tentacles into lands and villages all over the world."[25] King's words could not be more piercing given the fact that little has changed since he uttered them more than 40 years ago.

Illusions of progress are now often disguised as technological advances. With every new technological invention, plasma TV, smart phones, and 24-hour info-tainment, more and more the public feeds on stale bread of constant, nonstop information and entertainment and the lure of consumption. But in the shadows, the ranks of the poor are increasing and intensifying. As Gianni Vattimo, the Italian philosopher and critic of modernity has observed, technology as a reflection of modern thinking, gives the illusion of real progress.[26] However, King called on Americans to question their own material reality and to measure real progress by the elimination of poverty and make peace and nonviolence normative practices in local and global affairs. The gap between rich and poor is widening, where the concentration of wealth is becoming more magnified. According to Jeffrey Sachs,

- Each year, more than 8 million people around the world die because they are too poor to stay alive.
- Over 1 billion people—one in six people around the world—live in extreme poverty, defined as living on less than $1.00 a day.
- More than 800 million go hungry each day.
- Over 100 million primary school-age children cannot go to school.[27]

These statistical realities give new meaning to King's commitment to advance the beloved community as a continual process that seeks justice and affirms the dignity of all the world's citizens.

## Community through Social Action

Establishing the "beloved community" was not simply a teleological or eschatological hope. The beloved community was also in a state of becoming as individuals and groups of different races, classes, religious orientation, gender, and ethnicity worked together to make justice a reality for all people. One of the most powerful examples of community that King presented from his own life was during the Selma voting rights campaign of 1965. After he received the Nobel Peace Prize in Oslo the previous year, King returned to the United States with a renewed sense of vision and purpose. He approached the Selma campaign with a growing sense of urgency as he began to look toward issues of economic justice and criticism of the Vietnam War. Although his work in Selma proved to be one of his toughest challenges, it became a rallying cry for justice and reconciliation across the nation. For the first time in the civil rights movement, whites and blacks; Jews, Christians, and Muslims; the poor and well-to-do all descended on Selma to affirm freedom and justice for all. After two failed attempts at the march to shore up voting rights, it would have been easy for King to give up. Instead, with a central philosophy of nonviolence as the capstone of the movement on the line, King pursued a third and final "redemption" march where he called on the nation to descend on Selma for a peaceful protest. Under increasing criticism, as he tried to put his organization and the movement in Selma back on track, he commented to Governor Leroy Collins and Acting Assistant Attorney General John Doar in a private meeting: "I would rather die on the Highway in Alabama than make a butchery of my conscience by compromising with evil."[28]

Although King did not use the language of Empire explicitly, he saw the civil rights struggle as part of the unfolding of a cosmic drama of good triumphing over evil. Local demonstrations, such as the Selma march, were episodes of human beings working as colaborers with God to redeem human community, social systems, and a culture of violence. On March 25, 1965, King comforted and inspired a beaten down and wearied crowd of protestors as they marched from Selma's blood drenched Edmund Pettus Bridge to the capital city. From the steps of the capitol building in Montgomery, Alabama, described as "the Cradle of the Confederacy," King said:

> Once more the method of nonviolent resistance was unsheathed from its scabbard and once again an entire community was mobilized to confront the adversary. And again the brutality

of a dying order shrieks across the land. Yet, Selma, Alabama, became a shining moment in the conscience of man.[29]

There never was a moment in American history more honorable and more inspiring than the pilgrimage of clergymen and laymen of every race and faith pouring into Selma to face danger at the side of its embattled Negroes.[30]

Confrontation of good and evil compressed in the tiny community of Selma generated the massive power to turn the whole nation to a new course.[31]

He went on to say, with prophetic clarity, reflecting the profound sense of immediacy during the time:

Like an idea whose time has come, not even the marching of mighty armies can halt us. We are moving to the land of freedom. Let us therefore continue our triumph and march to the realization of the American dream.[32]

Our aim [he preached] must never be to defeat or humiliate the white man but to win his friendship and understanding. We must come to see that the end we seek is a society at peace with itself, a society that can live with its conscience.[33]

That sense of urgency continued as King moved toward the years of 1967 and 1968.

Taylor Branch, in the last of a trilogy of books on King and the civil rights movement, captures some of the contextual forces at work in the final days of King's life in his book, *At Canaan's Edge: America in the King Years 1965–1968*. Branch takes us back to the stormy day of February 1, 1968, when two sanitation workers squeezed in the back of a pushbutton trash collection compressor truck at the city dump because city rules restricted shelter stops in residential communities. After citizens complained about unsightly "picnics" by the Negro sanitation workers," black workers had little choices to avoid Memphis' torrential rains. When the foreman, Willie Crain, "heard the screams, he could not slam on the brakes, jump out, and disengage the pushbutton compressor fast enough."[34]

After King preached the sermon "The Drum Major Instinct" that Sunday, February 4, 1968, where he grappled with his own finitude and essentially expressed a heartfelt guide to his own funeral, he continued to maintain his outspoken criticism of the Vietnam War. King believed that his theological commitments to nonviolence and the ethical life of Jesus as the ultimate example, was not isolated to civil rights or a quest for economic justice, it was deeply related to a march of global militarism. At the same time, close friends and former supporters became more and more reticent about the use of nonviolence to enact social change. By now, some activists, like Stokely Carmichael and Floyd McKissick (both leaders in the Student Nonviolent Coordinating Committee [SNCC]), had grown weary in the struggle after at least ten years of nonviolent resistance. They began to question King's strategies and leadership. They joined with other black activists in the United States like Carmichael, Huey Newton, Angela Davis, and leaders in African countries, which included Ghana, Liberia, Kenya, and South Africa, to form what might be described as a Pan-African black militant resistance movement. Deeply saddened, King considered both the ramifications and strides accomplished since the civil rights movement galvanized people to act.

King, along with his travel aide Bernard Lee, returned to Memphis the morning of March 28, 1968. By now demonstrations were in full force as nearly one thousand sanitation workers began to march under the new slogan, "I AM A MAN" in honor of the slain workers. King's solidarity with Memphis sanitation workers reflected his radical shift from civil and voting rights to labor relations, militarism, and broader forces of economic justice. As he and Andrew Young, a former seminary student turned activist, planned for a 1969 Poor People's Campaign, along with King's call for a Bill of Rights for the poor, King became increasingly aware of the interconnectedness of war and poverty. In his final speech, "The Mountain Top," he provided a glimpse into his eschatological vision of justice and community. For King, the "promised land" reflected a grand historical struggle to overcome systemic racial, political, and economic injustice. On the eve of his April 3, 1968, assassination, King stepped in the pulpit at Mason Temple, headquarters of the Church of God in Christ, the largest African American Pentecostal denomination in the United States. Amid serious tornado warnings, with the clapping of storm shutters from the winds, which sounded like gun shots, King concluded:

> Well, I don't know what will happen now. We've got some difficult days ahead. But it doesn't matter with me now. Because I've been to the mountaintop. And I don't mind. Like anybody. I would like to live a long life. Longevity has its place. But I'm not concerned about that now. I just want to do God's will. And He's allowed me to go up to the mountain. And I've looked over. And I've seen the promised land. I may not get there with you. But I want you to know tonight, that we, as a people, will get to the promised land.[35]

Drawing on an ancient Hebrew exodus narrative, with images of the prophetic vision of Moses standing at the apex of Mount Nebo, King cast an imaginative image of peace and justice in an ever-changing world of difference and otherness.

His life and witness produced a global ethic of nonviolence, community and justice, which characterizes peace as not just the absence of conflict but the presence of justice. He inspired a whirlwind of global consciousness across the world, particularly in South Africa among many youth activists like Steven Biko, Nelson Mandela, Allan Boesak, and later a young Desmond Tutu. King's work continues to provide inspiration and hope to new generations as he made real the challenges of the global world in cities large and small throughout the country. King's vision of the beloved community sends a resounding message to us all today to urgently and courageously, join the struggle for freedom and human dignity at work today, from the slum villages of Cape Town, Nairobi and Port-a-Prince, to Mexico City, Tegucigulpa, Appalachia, and Indonesia. Indeed, there is much to do.

# 8

# Unlocking Doors of Hope: A Quest for Enduring Peace and Justice

More than 50 years ago, a man who dared to dream that the United States of America's "bank of justice"[1] is solvent became the youngest and the third person of African descent to receive the Nobel Peace Prize.[2] Approximately 45 years after the Reverend Dr. Martin Luther King Jr. accepted this award on behalf of the civil rights movement in the United States, Barack Hussein Obama, became "the third sitting United States president to be awarded the peace prize."[3] King dealt with the reality of inequality in a nation that marketed itself in 1964 as "the land of the free and the home of the brave"—a land where black people, poor people of all ethnicities, and women were denied basic liberties and rarely beneficiaries of often undisclosed legacy policies[4] that granted access to a select few that exacerbated disparities in education, employment, and housing.

King's acceptance speech described vividly the conditions of government sanctioned violence that black persons, and those who stood in solidarity with them, were subjected when they exercised their First Amendment right of free speech and collective protest.[5] King, recounting why he and countless others in "the United States of America are engaged in a creative battle to end the long night of racial injustice"[6] provided these details:

a) in Birmingham, Alabama, our children, crying out for brotherhood, were answered with fire hoses, snarling dogs and even death; b) in Philadelphia, Mississippi, young people seeking to secure the right to vote were brutalized and murdered; c) more than 40 houses of worship in the State of Mississippi alone were bombed or burned because they offered a sanctuary to those who would not accept segregation. (King, Nobel Peace Prize Acceptance Speech)

When King accepted this peace prize, the United States was also into its eighth year of what would become an almost twenty year military engagement in Viet Nam.

When Barack Obama, the first United States president of African descent, was sworn into office as the forty fourth president, he also assumed ultimate responsibility for actions that commenced in 2003 when a US-led military coalition invaded Iraq. Perhaps no one was more surprised than President Obama that he, "commander in chief of the military of a nation in the midst of two wars"[7] would be a recipient of a peace prize. As Obama shared with David Remnick, "It [the Nobel Prize for Peace] was not helpful to us politically...the one thing we didn't anticipate this year was having to apologize for having won the Nobel Peace Prize."[8] Or, as David Axelrod, in his capacity as senior advisor to the president acknowledged,

It's not necessarily an award he would have given himself. In that sense, it poses a challenge, but thinking through these issues is not burdensome. He spends a lot of time thinking about how you promote a more peaceful and secure world, about the appropriate use of power and about the value and importance of diplomacy. (Jeff Zeleny, "Accepting Peace Prize Will Be a Test for Obama")

Given ongoing debates about a reluctance of some publicly recognized leaders of the 1960s civil rights movement to "hand the baton" to a younger generation of leaders, we do not analyze Obama's speech as an apologetics for war.[9] Instead, we discuss how King's and Obama's Nobel Peace Prize speeches can serve as a basis from which to develop a response to current social issues. For us, a basic contention is that echoes of *dreams deferred*,[10] couched in a twenty-first century affirmative call-to-action of "yes we can",[11] cannot ignore the poignancy of King's description of the stark reality of 1964, as of 2013, "debilitating and grinding poverty afflicts my people and chains them to the lowest rung of the economic ladder."[12] This truth is a clarion reminder that while some citizens are "taxed enough already" a small percentage of persons who are perhaps not taxed enough with added benefits from tax loopholes suggests that a tendency to focus on an imagined middle class and an elite minority further obscures the plight of the poor.

## These Truths

Described by some as an "ambitious effort to address the problem of persistent poverty in the United Sates",[13] "President Lyndon B. Johnson declared a war on poverty in his 1964 State of the Union address, and Americans have been fighting a losing battle ever since."[14] Like its fictitious 1971 counterpart the War on Drugs, the War on Poverty was not designed to dismantle systems from which an elite few benefit financially nor to counter the *pull yourself up by your bootstraps* myth.[15] Programmatic mismanagement exacerbates a tendency to shift blame to the very people who are often ill equipped to navigate bureaucratic systems that objectify and commodify human beings. However, in spite of needed improvements that lend themselves to valuing the human dignity of all persons, government initiatives in the form of social safety nets can be a positive response to address life-negating conditions of the least of these in a country that self-markets itself as the wealthiest nation in the world. At the same time, adult recipients of Temporary Assistance for Needy Families (TANF) and Supplemental Nutritional Assistance Programs (SNAP), for example, are frequently characterized as lazy and increasingly dependent on the federal government for handouts while children, 23 percent of whom lived in families with income below the federal poverty level in 2012,[16] are often invisible and thus ignored.

This level of blind indifference suggests a literal understanding of a biblical injunction ascribed to Jesus that "you always have the poor with you, but you do not always have me."[17] This nonnuanced *a contextual* understanding refuses to consider an alternative biblical account that is coupled with a mandate that we "...can show kindness to them whenever we wish."[18] Thus, when we consider the plight of persons in a republic that markets itself as a democracy built on and sustained by an oligarchic capitalistic enterprise, how we treat the poor is often in stark contrast to entitlements bestowed upon the United States' wealthiest citizens. As we imagine Jesus' discussion with persons who participated actively in his community-based initiatives and witnessed his response to cultural norms, we posit that their reaction to a woman's appropriation of funds without first obtaining consent from Jesus' disciples inhibited their ability to fully comprehend what it means to care for others. They heard Jesus' words and yet missed the essence of his theological-anthropological truth claim. How we treat the poor is an indicator of our relationship with God whom we cannot see. What do we see? Who are the poor? How do we, individually and collectively, respond to the poor?

We contend that many assumed The Housing and Economic Recovery Act of 2008,[19] introduced by Representative Nancy Pelosi July 30, 2007 and signed by President George H. W. Bush a year later, was an indirect response to the poor. Yet, more than five years since its enactment, we continue to live in the shadow of a yet unfolding economic crisis. This fiscal and moral dilemma advantages banks designated too big to fail. As residential foreclosures and home values plummeted, congressional responses to persons who live with the residual effects of long-term unemployment or underemployment indicate an *a contextual* adoption of Bill Clinton's 1992 campaign assertion that "people who work hard and play by the rules shouldn't be poor"[20] without regard to who makes the rules by which people play. Peter Edelman, former assistant secretary for planning and evaluation at the Department of Health and Human Services who "resigned in protest over the new welfare law,"[21] was adamant that Bill Clintons' 1996 Personal Responsibility and Work Opportunity Act (PRWOA),

> is not welfare reform. It does not promote work effectively, and it will hurt millions of poor children by the time it is fully

implemented. What's more, it bars hundreds of thousands of legal immigrants – including many who have worked in the United States for decades and paid a considerable amount in Social Security and income taxes – from receiving disability and old-age assistance and food stamps, and reduces food-stamp assistance for millions of children in working families. (Edelman, "The Worst Thing Bill Clinton Has Done")

Edelman, a professor at Georgetown University Law Center, has advocated along with his spouse Marian Wright Edelman on behalf of children and families affected by poverty for decades.

Familiar with legislative processes, Edelman's characterization of the plight of poor persons in the United States is indicative of what King referred to as "the most pressing problem confronting mankind [sic] today...There is a sort of poverty of the spirit...we have not learned the simple art of living together as brothers [sic].[22] In 1964, as King stated, "at least one-fifth of our fellow citizens – some ten million families, comprising about forty million individuals – are bound to a miserable culture of poverty."[23] Less than a half-century later, consider the following census data on poverty in 2011:

- Overall poverty rate was 15.0 percent
- 16.1 million children (persons under 18) living in poverty
- Child poverty rate was 21.9 percent
- Poverty rate for African American children was 34.1 percent
- For non-Hispanic, White children the poverty rate was 12.5 percent
- Children living in female-headed families with no spouse present had a poverty rate of 47.6 percent
- Poverty rate for people age 65 and over was 8.7 percent
- 6.6 percent of all people, or 20.4 million people, lived in deep poverty[24]

Contrast this with a 2011 intention by select congressional members to reduce the debt.

A contingency of elected representatives propose, on the one hand, to reduce greatly programs designed to address the effects of poverty on children, such as food stamps.[25] On the other hand, these same congress members refuse to even consider legislation that would increase the tax rates for the superrich. The debt and poverty are, as Jon Healey opines,[26] both problems. We concur with Healey that

> Policymakers across the political spectrum wince at such statistics, and they agree that faster economic growth is a key part of the solution. They disagree sharply, though, on how to achieve it. Many Democrats argue that federal budget cuts are holding back growth, and that the GOP's efforts to reduce funding for food stamps and other entitlements will only punish the people hurt the most by the slack economy. Many Republicans counter that federal spending is impeding the vigorous economic growth that would reduce the demand for aid programs. (Healey, Federal debt still a problem, but so is poverty)

This stance, though, is predicated on a direct correlation between manufacturing and domestic employment.

We find this ironic when, even during the era dubbed the War on Terror, manufacturing jobs were outsourced outside the United States. Increasingly, the United States is shifting to (1) a service-based economy marked by low wages for the persons who are unable to enlist the services of a lobbyist to advocate on their behalf and (2) a money production economy marked by high wages for a few who underwrite political campaigns of policy makers. It is this dilemma of gross injustice that Edelman discussed in May 2012 interview.[27] According to Edelman,

> Fundamentally, our economy has been very unkind to the entire bottom half of our people over the last 40 years. We have terrific public policy in place, although it's threatened now by Paul Ryan, as you just showed. But we've done a lot, from Social Security, Medicare and Medicaid, to food stamps and the earned income tax credit. We're keeping more than 40 million people out of poverty now by the public policy that we have. But that's fighting against the flood of low-wage jobs that we've had over the last 40 years and the fact that people in the bottom half have been absolutely stuck, that the wages for people at the bottom have not—have grown only 7 percent over that 40-year period. So we're fighting uphill with the public policies that we have. It's

even harder for people who are—which is single moms in this economy, who are all by themselves in this low-wage economy trying to earn enough to support their children. It's very, very hard to do that with the flood of low-wage jobs that we have. (Edelman, Democracy Now!)

Poverty is, as King so aptly articulated, "one of the most urgent items on the agenda of modern life."[28] Yet if, as King insisted, "oppressed people cannot remain oppressed forever,"[29] we cannot ignore that in the last quarter of 2013 "the demand for dignity, equality, jobs, and citizenship will not be abandoned or diluted or postponed."[30]

King issued a moral call-to-action that requires us to consider how we appropriate varied points of privilege to confront systemic sins couched in xenophobic rhetoric. Will we, as King so boldly proclaimed in 1964, "not flinch...not be cowed...not be afraid"[31] to stand on the side of justice? Renewed calls to understand and apply constitutional rights compel us to consider how the plight of persons ensnared, for example, in global human trafficking networks influence our ability to grasp these and other documented truths. Our responses to these truths that are sustained by capitalistic enterprise are indicators of our moral compass.

## Audacious Faith

Given King's generational ties to the Black Church tradition, allow us to suggest, though we have no evidence to support this claim, that when he delivered his Nobel Peace Prize acceptance speech, the chorus of the spiritual "I Shall Not be Moved" reverberated in his soul.

> I shall not be, I shall not be moved;
> I shall not be, I shall not be moved;
> Just like a tree that's planted by the waters,
> Lord, I shall not be moved.[32]

The song's refrain captures what we refer to as audacious faith—an unwillingness to deny the exigencies of life as one engages in the work of justice.

King was resolute in his commitment to confront evil with a theologically informed human rights agenda. Although his approach was flawed by patriarchy and its associated societal ills, King was adamant that "there is nothing new about poverty. What is new, however, is that we have the resources to get rid of it."[33] What he proposed was not a war on poverty but "an all-out war against poverty."[34] In other words, nothing short of a dismantling of systems predicated on an economics of poverty would suffice to dispel myths that each US citizen is granted an equal opportunity to adequate housing, quality education, and health care.

King had the audacity to imagine a beloved community that resembles Nicholas Wolterstorff's vision of *shalom* that is "intertwined with justice."[35] For King and Wolterstorff, *shalom* is embodied in our actions on behalf of all persons and the environment. And it stands to reason this applies especially to our interaction with persons who are constructed and depicted as the *other*. With a faith informed commitment to active participation in God's always unfolding kingdom on earth, "in shalom, each person enjoys justice, enjoys his or her rights. There is no shalom without justice. Shalom is the human being dwelling at peace in all his or her relationships: with God, with self, with fellows, with nature."[36] *Shalom* is simultaneously a state of being and active engagement with the world that characterizes audacious faith.

As King explained, audacious faith refuses to accept "despair as the final response to the ambiguities of history."[37] Instead, audacious faith requires a type of sight that can imagine things as they should be and not as they are so that women, for instance, will not be subjected to draconian attempts to subvert reproductive rights. As King made clear, audacious faith rejects the idea that "the view that mankind [sic] is so tragically bound to the starless midnight of racism and war that the bright daybreak of peace and brotherhood [sic] can never become a reality."[38] Instead, with unrestrained imagination, audacious faith beckons us to name unambiguously evil cloaked in politically acceptable rhetoric. Audacious faith demands an accurate interpretation of calls to *take back our country,* so that we do not unconsciously succumb to dehumanizing practices. Audacious faith reminds us that a call to remember is a theological ethical mandate that enables us to move forward as we purpose to value all of God's children.

When we reflect on an emerging anti-intellectual sentiment that can be traced, in part, publicly to the 2008 Republican Vice Presidential candidate, Sarah Palin, audacious faith in the twenty-first century demands that we remember that less than 150 years ago it was illegal for persons of African descent to read and write in the United States. By contrast, King had "the audacity to believe peoples everywhere can have three meals a day for their bodies, education and culture for their minds, and dignity, equality and freedom for their spirits."[39] Audacious faith in contemporary times must draw attention to de facto segregation that results in educational disparity that leaves more than one child too ill prepared to engage in public life or contribute to the common good. As Pell Grants continue to decrease almost proportionately in relation to increases in tuition, audacious faith demands that we not envision higher education as an elite privilege but rather as an avenue by which many are granted access to *dream a world* where their ideas are essential to influencing decisions that affect the well-being of the world's population.

By thinking expansively, audacious faith reminds us, as King remarked, "that in the final analysis, the rich must not ignore the poor because both rich and poor are tied in a single garment of destiny."[40] This suggests that careful attention must be given to the manner in which moral issues are depicted in the media. With audacious faith, we hone our ability to discern undisclosed motives and in so doing identify strategies that lend themselves to fostering spaces where the superrich might indeed be able to acknowledge the full humanity of impoverished persons. At the same time, instead of an uninformed naïveté, this commitment to justice is couched in a form of realistic pragmatism that demands an ongoing assessment of human relations. In other words, audacious faith takes seriously a mandate to treat others in a manner that reflects our relation with the divine. Persons with audacious faith, believe as King did, that doers of justice

- Take direct action against injustice despite the failure of governmental and other official agencies to act first
- Do not obey unjust laws or submit to unjust practices
- Persuade without resorting to violence
- Seek as an ultimate goal a community at peace with itself
- Will always be willing to talk and seek fair compromise
- Will suffer when necessary and even risk their lives to become witnesses to truth as we see it (King, "The Quest for Peace and Justice")

Informed by the lived reality of persons whose humanity is subjected to gross disregard, often based on factors outside their control, audacious faith suggests that we must cultivate a hope that even if God does not respond as we desire that we will continue to persist in our efforts ever mindful that God is yet with us.

## Audacious Hope

Audacious hope, an ability to imagine life unencumbered by governmental sanctioned atrocities, can emerge from an incubator that is forged in historical remembrances. King realized, even as he and others were met with high-powered fire hoses, attack dogs, and other weapons of human destruction in the 1960s, that "every crisis has both its dangers and its opportunities."[41] In a context where people were assigned value based on socially manufactured notions of race, King stood on the steps of the Lincoln Memorial on the centennial remembrance of the signing of the Emancipation Proclamation and declared that freedom was still an illusion for one too many African diasporic people. The poignant relevance of his insight at the March on Washington for Jobs and Freedom is all too often loss on an overemphasis by some, who would otherwise not be proponents of his proposals, on a dream devoid of critical thought coupled with responsible action.

King, voicing a truth claim reminiscent of W. E. B. Du Bois' classic description of life as a black United Statesian,[42] stated that the more than two-hundred thousand persons gathered in the nation's capital were there primarily "to dramatize a shameful condition."[43] In this regard, audacious hope encourages persons to give voice to previously silenced recollections that offer a counter narrative to life in the United States. Audacious hope serves to remind us, as King so aptly asserted, that "the problem of poverty is not only seen in the class division between the highly developed industrial nations and the so-called underdeveloped nations; it is seen in the great economic gaps within the rich nations themselves."[44] It is this socioeconomic disparity that, to some degree, influences Obama's desire to overhaul the health-care system.

With genealogical roots in Kansas and Kenya, Obama spent his formative years in Hawaii and Indonesia. At issue for some presidential dissenters is the question of Obama's citizenship. Some suggest that his birth certificate is fraudulent. Others insist that even if he was born in Hawaii, that Obama declared dual citizenship in Kenya. This and a myriad of other ideas fuel Birthers'[45] initiatives in Obama's second term as president, to raise doubts about his country of birth as potential grounds for impeachment. Amazingly, Obama is not swayed publicly by allegations that he is not a legitimate holder of the highest elected office in the United States. Barack Hussein Obama garners both praise and criticism for his willingness, or lack thereof, to challenge assumptions about what constitutes hope. For instance, the repeal of the Defense of Marriage Act (DOMA) and "Don't Ask, Don't Tell" (DADT) signal hope to countless individuals that life, liberty, and the pursuit of happiness can be more than an illusion.

Although evidence related to the success or failure of his signature legislature, The Affordable Care Act: Secure Health Coverage for the Middle Class,[46] is mixed during the initial launch of the program's website, we do applaud the fact that:

- Insurance companies no longer have unchecked power to cancel your policy, deny your child coverage due to a preexisting condition, or charge women more than men.
- Over 86 million Americans have gained from coverage of preventive care free of charge, like mammograms for women and wellness visits for seniors.

- The law has helped 6.6 million young adults who have been able to stay on their parents' plans until the age of 26, including 3.1 million young people who are newly insured.[47]

In spite of this, the description of this Act to "ensure hard-working, middle class families will get the security they deserve"[48] serves as a cautionary reminder that vigilance is still necessary to "protect every American from the worst insurance company abuses."[49] This nomenclature conflates health insurance, which is in dire need of reform, and health care, whose access and quality is often contingent on a patient's ability to pay.

It is this moral dilemma, an ability to acquire health insurance and not have the financial means to obtain quality care, that presents as a possibility to address something that is difficult but is an ethical possibility that can be achieved. Herein lies a glimmer of hope in Obama's Nobel Prize lecture. If we apply his lessons on war to domestic policies, in this case, health-care coverage, we too concede that, "for all the cruelty and hardship of our world, we are not mere prisoners of fate. Our actions matter, and can bend history in the direction of justice."[50] What might it take to guarantee health care, especially preventive services, to every person, regardless of residency status, who self identifies as a United Statesian? We contend that it is possible that the Affordable Care Act can serve as a primary vehicle by which medical practitioners will not discriminate based on patients' insurance carrier. It is admittedly possible that future revisions to Obama's signature legislation could address malpractice protocol. As an act of audacious hope, this would lead to a reduction in business expenses and patient costs as well as an increased emphasis on research and development.

## Can We? Yes, We Must

In the land of the free and the brave called the United States of America, we live daily with the consequences of greed, avarice, and hubris. Obama is absolutely correct that "security does not exist where human beings do not have access to enough food, or clean water, or the medicine and shelter they need to survive. It does not exist where children can't aspire to a decent education or a job that supports a family. The absence of hope can rot a society from within."[51] Interestingly though, there are creative personal and collective responses, which offer irrefutable proof that we can. Thus, it is imperative that we continue to embody principles that signal until every person is treated with dignity our verbal proclamations are little more than a "noisy gong or a clanging cymbal".[52] After all, as Obama posited, "for all the cruelty and hardship of our world, we are not mere prisoners of fate. Our actions matter and can bend history in the direction of justice."[53] In this age of Obama, in the shadow of King, "we can no longer afford to worship the God of hate or bow before the altar of retaliation. The oceans of history are made more turbulent by the ever-rising tides of hate. History is cluttered with the wreckage of nations and individuals that pursued this self-defeating path of hate. Love is the key to the solution of the problems of the world."[54] For us, love is not an abstract concept cloaked in religious language.

Love in its deeper significance, a concept that is often central to a Christian understanding of koinonia or community, is essential to the church's ongoing reformation and participation in the world. From King's prophetic declarations and Obama's hope-filled refrain can emerge a reformation that is tantamount to an overturning of things as they are. By thinking expansively, people with access can appropriate varied points of privilege such that all can be housed, fed, clothed, and educated. For such a time as this, where elected officials are more concerned about protecting corporate donors' profit margins with little regard to advance the well being of the most vulnerable individuals, King and Obama remind us that a quest for enduring peace and justice necessitates that we take creative approaches to unlock doors of hope.

It is only when life-affirming behavior and rhetoric align that we share with God in acts of creation that unlock doors of hope. We realize that a quest for enduring peace and justice is a life-long endeavor. Nevertheless, we assert that it is a journey that challenges us to remember that war is not the absence of military engagement. A commitment to lasting peace and justice is a call-to-action that does not privilege one form of violence over another. Increased gun-related incidents in the United States are for us, of equal concern as oppressive regimes that are ignored and/or supported by this country. Prophetic voices, incarnated in churches, para-church ministries, not-for-profit organization, community- organizations, and countless individuals around the globe remind us that positive change occurs one person at a time. King dared to dream a dream and in so doing changed the course of history. We can, when we realize the power in collective truth, unlock doors of hope that will signal our commitment to peace and justice.

# Conclusion

On August 28, 1963, the Rev. Dr. Martin Luther King, Jr. delivered his now infamous speech "I Have a Dream" in Washington, DC. Thousands gathered at the Lincoln Memorial and adjacent areas surrounding the reflecting pool to hear this scholar-pastor utter a prophetic word in a nation that used social constructions of race, class, and gender to justify systems of injustice. Because King had demonstrated an ability to speak truth to power during his involvement with the Montgomery, Alabama bus boycott individuals traveled miles to witness this historic 1963 event. Almost a decade since the Supreme Court's school desegregation ruling, attending the March on Washington meant that some individuals made a conscious decision to ride in segregated buses and trains. Individuals who elected to drive did so with the knowledge that they would have limited access to restaurants and public facilities, such as lavatories. In addition, families and community members who sacrificed to send a representative to the nation's capital gathered around televisions and radios to listen to this future Nobel Peace Prize winner (December 1964) declare unequivocally the full humanity of all people. On August 28, 1963, King challenged this country's citizens to consider the various ways in which social systems distorted concepts of the common good. He also challenged Americans to engage in a critical analysis at both an individual and corporate level in order to make a commitment to accept people based on their character and not a superficial trait.

Forty-five years later, on Thursday, August 28, 2008, in Denver, Colorado, Barack Hussein Obama—his father a Kenyan and his mother a Caucasian from Kansas—accepted the Democratic Party's presidential nomination. Just as many gathered in Washington, DC in 1963 to hear King, delegates from the 50 states, the America Samoa, Guam and Puerto Rica and thousands others witnessed this historic event in Invesco Field. While Sims acknowledges she was not a staunch Obama supporter, she indicates that she found herself overwhelmed on Wednesday, August 27, 2008, when Senator Hillary Clinton of New York, herself a former Democratic presidential candidate and the first female to win a significant number of primaries/caucuses, called for an acclimation during the roll call of states. It was at that moment that Sims began to wonder if the United States of America was at a point where we could truly look beyond surface differences—pigmentation—and elect someone based on their ability to make a positive difference.

In the midst of an economic crisis with global implications, then Senator Obama invited United Statesians, irrespective of political party affiliation, ethnic identity, socioeconomic status, or a myriad of social constructions, to begin to imagine hope-filled possibilities. Whether it was his message—yes you can—or a combination of factors both within and outside his influence and/or control, the 2008 presidential campaign echoed the hope in Martin King's "I Have a Dream Speech" and the promise of possibilities reflected in President Obama's election. At the same time, we are adamant that we cannot ignore the complicated dialogues associated with the election of a black man that challenge us to reexamine the ways in which language colors and shapes public opinion.

We complete our collaborative writing endeavor approximately one year after President Obama began his second term of office. Wars, civil unrest, and gross inequities abound. Ideas about what constitutes the common good, disguised by a skillful deployment of rhetoric and minimum regard for "fact checking" leave us with more questions than answers. An inept congress, with elected republican representatives unashamedly adamant that their primary goal, after an unsuccessful bid to "take back" the White House in 2012, is to work to dismantle government-sponsored social service programs, epitomizes dysfunction, and is the anathema of John Rawls' concept of justice as fairness.

Given the vast numbers of uninsured, unemployed, and under employed persons, rather than repeated attempts to overturn the Affordable Health Care Act, aka Obama Care, we question why an increasing number of elected officials are unable to set aside partisan differences and engage in a serious dialogue on matters of democracy that may, even if only in some very measurable way, embody principles that do not unfairly privilege a select group of persons and corporations who own and control more than 85 percent of this country's wealth.

In his sermon "The Audacity to Hope," which inspired President Obama's 2008 book *The Audacity of Hope: Thoughts on Reclaiming the American Dream*, Jeremiah Wright invites us to consider what is at stake in "a world that cares more about bombs for the enemy than bread for the hungry."[1] The first presidential debate on October 3, 2012, left us grappling for hope as we continue to stand in solidarity with the disenfranchised, the homeless, the unauthorized, the undocumented, the incarcerated, the uninsured, the "47%" and the "30%" who are, in every sense of the way, us. As we look toward tomorrow, may we purpose "to hope when the love of God is not plainly evident"[2] ever mindful of a prophetic proclamation "to do good, to love justice, and to walk humbly with the Divine".

# Notes

## Preface

1. Trinity United Church of Christ's self-identity honors a history of struggle by blacks whose ability to engage in contextual biblical exegesis that gave voice to particularities that distinguished slaveholding religion from a nascent form of liberation theology in the United States. For information on the Black Value System that informs Trinity's collective sense of a people who believe that God meets us in the particularity of our situation, see http://www.trinitychicago.org/index.php?option=com_content&task=view&id=114 (accessed September 22, 2013).
2. Kelly Brown Douglas describes white culture as a pathology that undergirds normative constructions in the United States. See *Sexuality and the Black Church: A Womanist Perspective* (Maryknoll, NY: Orbis, 1999).
3. Regina Wang, "Billy Graham No Longer Thinks Mormonism Is a Cult," http://newsfeed.time.com/2012/10/19/billy-graham-no-longer-thinks-mormonism-is-a-cult/ (accessed October 4, 2013).
4. Philip Rucker, "Mitt Romney Opens Up about Mormonism," http://www.washingtonpost.com/blogs/post-politics/wp/2013/04/30/mitt-romney-opens-up-about-mormonism/ (accessed October 4, 2013).
5. Donald L. Ashton, "Mormon Doctrine What's Official, and What Isn't?" http://www.staylds.com/docs/WhatIsOfficialMormonDoctrine.html (accessed October 4, 2013).

## I   Not God Bless America, God Damn America: Black Rhetorical Performance and Patriotic Idealism

1. Helen T. Gray, "A Prophet in His Own Land," *The Kansas City Star*, March 29, 2008, E14 and E12.
2. Alan Geyer, "Patriotism," in *The Westminster Dictionary of Christian Ethics*, James F. Childress and John Macquarrie, ed. (Philadelphia: Westminster, 1986), 452.

3. See, for example, Toby Harnden, "Does White America Hate Obama?" *The Daily Telegraph* (London), September 17, 2009; Stanley Kurtz, "'Context' You Say?" *National Review*, May 19, 2008; Marty Wiseman, "We May no Longer Avoid the Race Issue, So Let's Talk," *Mississippi Business Journal*, March 31–April 6, 2008; and Transcript of then Senator Barack Obama's March 18, 2008, Speech, http://www.npr.org/templates/story/story.php?storyId=88478467 (accessed April 1, 2013).

4. For additional information on discourse analysis, see Norman Fairclough, *Analysing Discourse: Textual Analysis for Social Research* (London: Routledge, 2003); Carmen Rosa Caldas-Coulthard and Malcolm Coulthard, eds., *Texts and Practices: Readings in Critical Discourse Analysis* (London: Routledge, 1996); Bethan Benwell and Elizabeth Stokoe, *Discourse and Identity* (Edinburgh: Edinburgh University Press, 2006); Mary Talbot, *Media Discourse: Representation and Interaction* (Edinburgh: Edinburgh University Press, 2007); Mary Christine Banwart, "Constructing Images in Presidential Primaries: An Analysis of Discourse Strategies in the Dole and Bush Iowa Straw Poll Speeches." *Argumentation and Advocacy* 43, no. 2 (2006).

5. Geyer, "Patriotism," 452.

6. Edward S. Herman, professor emeritus of finance at the Wharton School of Business, and David Peterson, a Chicago-based independent journalist and researcher analyze statistical data to examine media's pattern with coverage of Wright and minimum attention given to views of Caucasian pastors during the 2008 presidential campaign. See "Jeremiah Wright in the Propaganda System." *Monthly Review* 60, no. 04 (September 2008), http://www.monthlyreview.org/080901herman-peterson.php (accessed June 29, 2013).

7. Geyer, "Patriotism," 452.

8. W. E. B. Du Bois, *The Negro Church*, with an Introduction by Alton B. Pollard II (Eugene, OR: Cascade, 2011).

9. Du Bois, *The Negro Church*, 12.

10. In addition to Du Bois, see Susanna Delfino and Michele Gillespie, eds., *Neither Lady nor Slave: Working Women of the Old South* (Chapel Hill, NC: University of North Carolina Press, 2002); Charles F. Irons, *The Origins of Proslavery Christianity: White and Black Evangelicals in Colonial and Antebellum Virginia* (Chapel Hill, NC: University of North Carolina Press, 2008); Lester B. Scherer, *Slavery and the Churches in Early America, 1619–1819* (Grand Rapids, MI: William B. Eerdmans Publishing, 1975).

11. For a description of religious experience of slaves, see Albert J. Raboteau, *Slave Religion: The "Invisible Institution" in the Antebellum South* (New York: Oxford University Press, 2004).

12. Walter Brueggemann, "Biblical Authority," *Moral Issues & Christian Responses*, 8th edition, Patricia Beattie Jung and L. Shannon Jung, ed. (Minneapolis, MN: Fortress, 2012).

13. For a brief description see Anne H. Pinn and Anthony B. Pinn, *Introduction to Black Church History* (Minneapolis, MN: Fortress, 2001).

14. For information on Gilbert Tennent, see Dennis Barone, "James Logan and Gilbert Tennent: Enlightened Classicist Versus Awakened Evangelist." *Early American Literature,* 21 (1986): 103–117; Milton J. Coalter, Jr., "The Radical Pietism of Count Nicholas Zinzendorf as a Conservative Influence on the Awakener, Gilbert Tennent." *Church History,* 49 (1980): 35–46 and *Gilbert Tennent, Son of Thunder: A Case Study of Continental Pietism's Impact on the First Great Awakening in the Middle Colonies* (Westport, CT: Greenwood Press, 1986); Janet F. Fishburn, "Gilbert Tennent, Established "Dissenter."" *Church History* 63 (1994): 31–49.

15. Fishburn, "Gilbert Tennent, Established "Dissenter,"" 36.

16. Barone, "James Logan and Gilbert Tennent," 103–117.

17. Ibid., 106 and 109.

18. Julius H. Rubin, *Religious Melancholy and Protestant Experience in America* (New York: Oxford University Press, 1994), 91.

19. See Barone, "James Logan and Gilbert Tennent"; Coalter, "The Radical Pietism of Count Nicholas Zinzendorf"; and Fishburn, "Gilbert Tennent, Established "Dissenter.""

20. Barone, "James Logan and Gilbert Tennent," 111.

21. Ibid., 111.

22. Ibid.

23. Ibid.

24. Ibid.

25. Fishburn, "Gilbert Tennent, Established "Dissenter,"" 49.

26. Ibid., 40.

27. See Barone, "James Logan and Gilbert Tennent"; Coalter, "The Radical Pietism of Count Nicholas Zinzendorf"; and Fishburn, "Gilbert Tennent, Established "Dissenter.""

28. For information on Charles Grandison Finney, see Frank Grenville Beardsley, *A Mighty Winner of Souls: Charles G. Finney a Study in Evangelism* (New York, NY: American Tract Society, 1937); David B. Chesebrough, *Charles G. Finney: Revivalistic Rhetoric* (Westport, CT: Greenwood Press, 2001); Keith J. Hardman, *Charles Grandison Finney, 1792–1875: Revivalist and Reformer* (Syracuse, NY: Syracuse University Press, 1987); William G. McLoughlin, ed., *Lectures on Revivals of Religion by Charles Grandison Finney* (Cambridge, MA: The Belknap Press of Harvard University Press, 1960); William G. McLoughlin, "Charles Grandison Finney: The Revivalist as Culture Hero." *Journal of American Culture 5,* no 2(Summer 1983): 80–90; Marianne Perciaccante, *Calling Down Fire: Charles Grandison Finney and Revivalism in Jefferson County, New York, 1800–1840* (Albany, NY: State University of New York Press, 2003).

29. For information on Dwight Lyman Moody, see Bruce J. Evensen, *God's Man for the Gilded Age: D. L. Moody and the Rise of Modern Mass Evangelism* (New York, NY: Oxford University Press, 2003); James F. Findlay Jr., *Dwight L. Moody: American Evangelists 1837–1899* (Chicago, IL: The University of Chicago Press, 1969); H. M. Wharton, *A Month with Moody: His Work and Workers* (Baltimore: Wharton & Barron Publishing Co., 1893).

30. For an analysis of Finney's evangelistic approach, see Edwin S. Gustad, "Charles Grandison Finney: Revivalism." *Mid-Stream* 8, no 3 (Spring 1969): 80–91.

31. See William G. McLoughlin, "Charles Grandison Finney: The Revivalist as Culture Hero." *Journal of American Culture* 5, no 2 (Summer 1983): 80–90.

32. See Beardsley, *A Mighty Winner of Souls*; Chesebrough, *Charles G. Finney*; Hardman, *Charles Grandison Finney, 1792–1875*; McLoughlin, "Charles Grandison Finney"; and Perciaccante, *Calling Down Fire*.

33. See Ethan Acres, "Toup Dreams." *Art Issues* 59 (September/October 1999): 33–39; David W. Bebbington, "How Moody Changed Revivalism." *Christian History* 9, no. 1 (1990): 22–25; Bruce J. Evensen, "'The Greatest Day That Our City Has Ever Seen': Moody, Medill, and Chicago's Gilded Age Revival." *Journal of Media & Religion* 1, no. 4 (2002): 231–249.

34. See Bruce J. Evensen, ""Expecting a Blessing of Unusual Magnitude": Moody, Mass Media, and Gilded Age Revival." *Journalism History* 24, no. 1 (Spring 1998): 26–36; "'It is a Marvel to Many People': Dwight L. Moody, Mass Media, and the New England Revival of 1877." *New England Quarterly* 72, no. 2 (June 1999): 251–274; and ""Saucepan Journalism" in an Age of Indifference: Moody, Beecher, and Brooklyn's Gilded Press." *Journalism History* 27, no. 4 (Winter 2001/2002):165–177. Timothy George, "Why We Still Need Moody." *Christianity Today* 43, no. 14 (December 6, 1999): 66–68.

35. See David Mass, "The Life & Times of D. L. Moody." in *Christian History* 9, no. 1 (1990): 5–11.

36. See Evensen, *It is a Marvel to Many People*; Findlay, *Dwight L. Moody*; and Wharton, *A Month with Moody*.

37. For a regional example see Douglas Firth Anderson, "San Francisco Evangelicalism, Regional Religious Identity, and the Revivals of D L Moody." *Fides et Historia* 15, no. 2 (Spring/Summer 1983): 44–66.

38. See Beardsley, *A Mighty Winner of Souls*; Chesebrough, *Charles G. Finney*; Hardman, *Charles Grandison Finney, 1792–1875*; McLoughlin, "Charles Grandison Finney"; and Perciaccante, *Calling Down Fire*.

39. For information on Henry Ward Beecher, see Lyman Abbott, *Henry Ward Beecher* (Charleston, SC: Nabu Press, 2010); Debby Applegate, *The Most Famous Man in America: The Biography of Henry Ward Beecher* (New York, NY: Three Leaves Press, 2006); John Henry Barrows, *Henry*

*Ward Beecher: The Shakespeare of the Pulpit* (New York, NY: Funk & Wagnalls Company, 1893); William C. Beecher and Rev. Samuel Scoville, assisted by Mrs. Henry Ward Beecher, *A Biography of Rev. Henry Ward Beecher* (New York, NY: Charles L. Webster & Company, 1888); Clifford E. Clark Jr., *Henry Ward Beecher: Spokesman for a Middle-Class America* (Urbana, IL: University of Illinois Press, 1978); Joseph Howard Jr., *Life of Henry Ward Beecher* (Philadelphia, PA: Hubbard Brothers Publishers, 1887); Thomas W. Knox, *Life and Work of Henry Ward Beecher* (Philadelphia, PA: Bradley & Company, 1887); Lyman Abbott, *Henry Ward Beecher as His Friends Saw Him.* https://archive. org/details/henrywardbeecher00bost (accessed January 31, 2014).

40. For Beecher's stance on human rights, see Frank Decker, "Working as a Team: Henry Ward Beecher and the Plymouth Congregation in the Anti-Slavery Cause." *International Congregational Journal* 8, no. 2 (Fall 2009): 33–42; Wayne Shaw, "The Plymouth Pulpit: Henry Ward Beecher's Slave Auction Block." *ATQ* 14, no. 4 (December 2000): 335–343.

41. See Abbott, *Henry Ward Beecher*; Applegate, *The Most Famous Man*; Barrows, *Henry Ward Beecher*; Beecher and Scoville, *A Biography*; Clark, *Henry Ward Beecher*; Howard, *Life*; Knox, *Life and Work*; and Tewksbury, *Henry Ward Beecher.*

42. Ibid.

43. Ibid.

44. Ibid.

45. Charles H. Long, September 5, 2008 e-mail.

46. Traci C. West, *Disruptive Christian Ethics: When Racism and Women's Lives Matter* (Louisville, KY: Westminster John Knox, 2006), 57.

47. West, *Disruptive Christian Ethics,* 57.

48. For information on Martin Luther King Jr., see Lewis V. Baldwin, "The Unfolding of the Moral Order: Rufus Burrow, Jr., Personal Idealism, and the Life and Thought of Martin Luther King, Jr." *Pluralist* 6, no. 1 (Spring 2011): 1–13 and *The Voice of Conscience: The Church in the Mind of Martin Luther King, Jr.* (New York, NY: Oxford University Press, 2010); Rufus Burrow Jr., "The Beloved Community: Martin Luther King, Jr. and Josiah Royce." *Encounter* 73, no. 1 (Fall 2012): 37–64; David J. Garrow, *Bearing the Cross: Martin Luther King, Jr., and the Southern Christian Leadership Conference* (New York: Vintage Books, 1986); Karen V. Guth, "Reconstructing Nonviolence: The Political Theology of Martin Luther King Jr. after Feminism and Womanism." *Journal of the Society of Christian Ethics* 32, no. 1 (Spring/Summer 2012): 75–92; Jay-Paul Hinds, "The Prophet's Wish: A Freudian Interpretation of Martin Luther King's Dream." *Pastoral Psychology* 61, no. 4 (August 2012): 467–484; Martin Luther King, Jr., *A Testament of Hope: The Essential Writings and Speeches of Martin Luther King, Jr.* James M. Washington, ed. (New York, NY: HarperCollins, 1986); Cleophus J.

LaRue, "Two Ships Passing in the Night," in *What's the Matter with Preaching Today?* Mike Graves, ed. (Louisville, KY: Westminstr John Knox, 2004); David L. Lewis, *King: A Biography,* 2nd ed. (Urbana, IL: University of Illinois Press, 1978); Richard Lischer, *The Preacher King: Martin Luther King, Jr. and the Word That Moved America* (New York, NY: Oxford University Press, 1995); Stephen B. Oates, *Let the Trumpet Sound: A Life of Martin Luther King, Jr.* (New York: HarperPerennial, 1994); Bruce Worthington, "Martin Luther King Jr. as Identificatory Conglomerate." *Black Theology: An International Journal* 11, no. 2 (2013): 219–239.

49. Martin Luther King, Jr., "Why I Am Opposed to the War in Vietnam," http://www.lib.berkeley.edu/MRC/pacificaviet/riversidetranscript.html (accessed June 29, 2013).

50. Ibid.

51. Lischer, *The Preacher King,* 116.

52. Ibid., 8.

53. Ibid., 94.

54. See LaRue's summary discussion on black preaching methodology, "Two Ships Passing in the Night," 135–137.

55. Lischer, *The Preacher King,* 37.

56. Ibid., 95.

57. Ibid., 201.

58. Ibid., 4.

59. Ibid., 150.

60. Ibid., 210.

61. Ibid., 265.

62. Ibid., 221–242.

63. Ibid., 102.

64. Ibid., 141.

65. See Baldwin, "The Unfolding"; Garrow, *Bearing the Cross*; Lewis, *King*; Lischer *The Preacher King*; and Oates, *Let the Trumpet Sound.*

66. Ibid., 6.

67. Ibid., 219.

68. Ibid.

69. Ibid., 163.

70. See LaRue, "Two Ships Passing in the Night," 127.

71. Ibid., 253.

72. See Baldwin, "The Unfolding"; Garrow, *Bearing the Cross*; Lewis, *King*; Lischer *The Preacher King*; and Oates, *Let the Trumpet Sound.*

73. Ibid., 174.

74. Ibid., 177.

75. See Baldwin, "The Unfolding"; Garrow, *Bearing the Cross*; Lewis, *King*; Lischer *The Preacher King*; and Oates, *Let the Trumpet Sound.*

76. Ibid., 193.

77. Ibid., 12.

78. See Baldwin, "The Unfolding"; Garrow, *Bearing the Cross*; Lewis, *King*; Lischer *The Preacher King*; and Oates, *Let the Trumpet Sound*.

# 2   Disturbing the Peace: Theological Mandate to Construct an Inclusive Vision of Humanity

1. The Most Ridiculous Anti-Obama Signs, http://politicalhumor.about.com/library/bl-anti-obama-signs.htm?ps=572%3A1 (accessed October 17, 2013).
2. www.ep.tc (accessed October 17, 2013).
3. Some believe the modern day political group named the Tea Party began on December 16, 2007 when Ron Paul used this day to raise funds for his presidential campaign. Please see Cynthia Holder Rich "Race, Religion, and Politics, Then and Now: The Copperheads and the Tea Party." *Sopher Press* 2, no. 3 (January 2011): 15–16.
4. Valerie Doane, "Life, Liberty and Pursuit of Happiness," *timesunion.com*, June 11, 2010, http://blog.timesunion.com/teaparty/date/2010/06/page/3/ (accessed October 17, 2013).
5. Holder, "Race, Religion, and Politics," 15.
6. Adams relies on John Locke for his treatise and development of these ideas.
7. Samuel Adams, "The Rights of the Colonists: Report of the Committee of Correspondence of the Boston Town Meeting, November 20, 1772," in *Old South Leaflets*, no. 173 (Boston: Directors of the Old South Work, 1906), http://history.hanover.edu/texts/adamss.html (accessed September 20, 2013.) Adams keeps the original language of Locke's use of property in his treatise. Locke used this phrase in his Second Treatise Concerning Civil Government. Locke also did use the language of happiness in his "Essays Concerning Human Understanding" (Book 2, Chapter 21, Section 51). The language of happiness is not foreign to Locke. Jefferson, who read Locke, changes the phrase in the Declaration from property to the pursuit of happiness.
8. Ibid.
9. Ibid.
10. Tea Party Not a Racists Organization, http://www.foxnews.com/politics/2010/07/18/tea-party-racist-organization-biden-says/ (accessed January 31, 2014).
11. Adams, "Rights of Colonists," Section III.
12. Ibid.
13. Ibid.
14. Ibid.
15. Ibid., Section I.
16. Dwight N. Hopkins, *Being Human: Race, Culture and Religion* (Minneapolis, MN: Fortress Press, 2005), 5.

17. Ibid., 6.
18. http://firstread.msnbc.msn.com/_news/2011/01/19/5879060-tea-party-freshman-invokes-chains-of-obamacare (accessed February 9, 2013).
19. Frederick Douglass, "The Meaning of July Fourth for the Negro," in *The Life and Writings of Frederick Douglass*, volume 2, Philip S. Foner, ed. (New York: International Publishers, 1975), 196.
20. Ibid.
21. Ibid., 202.
22. Ibid., 192.
23. Ibid., 190.
24. "10 Most Offensive Tea Party Signs and Extensive Photo Coverage from Tax Day Protests." (See particularly, "Barrach Hussein Obama The New Face of Hitler," keeping alive many of the negative stereotypes about President Obama) www.huffingtonpost.com/2009/04/16/10-most-of-fensive-tea-par_n_187554.html (accessed October 17, 2013).
25. Douglass, "The Meaning of July Fourth for the Negro," 200.
26. Ibid., 192.
27. Ibid., 201.
28. Frederick Douglass, "The Present and Future of the Colored Race in America," in *The Life and Writings of Frederick Douglass*, volume 3, Philip S. Foner, ed. (New York: International Publishers, 1975), 352.
29. Ibid.
30. Ibid.
31. Ibid.
32. Ibid.
33. Douglass, "The Present and Future of the Colored Race in America," 353.
34. Ibid., 354.
35. Ibid.
36. Ibid., 355.
37. Ibid.
38. Ibid.
39. Ibid.
40. Ibid., 356.
41. Ibid.
42. Ibid.
43. Ibid., 359.
44. Ibid.
45. This speech was delivered in the Church of the Puritans in New York, May 1863.
46. Hopkins, *Being Human*, Chapters 2–4.
47. Ibid., 81.
48. Ibid., 82.
49. Ibid.
50. Ibid., 83.

51. Ibid.
52. Ibid.
53. Ibid., 86.
54. Ibid.
55. Ibid.
56. Ibid., 93–94.
57. Ibid., 110.
58. Ibid., 109.
59. www.worldnews.sheardnow.com/tea-party-outraged-over-obamcare /3276/ (Carroll Sorrell, Tea Party Summit October 8, 2010).
60. Hopkins gives a detailed explanation of how he understands culture beginning on page 56 and continuing to 60. A key component for Hopkins is helping readers to understand that the material and spiritual are connected in what we call culture (pp. 56–57).
61. Hopkins, *Being Human*, 56.
62. Ibid.
63. Ibid., 78. The categories are: (1) politics (power to decide sharing and distributing resources), (2) aesthetics (dealing with proportions and forms of beauty), (3) kinship (the basic primary relations in society—the family), (4) recreation (relaxation and renewal of self and selves), (5) religion (worldviews and human relations around ultimate visions), and (6) ethics (values of right and wrong).
64. Ibid.
65. Ibid., 79.
66. Ibid.
67. Ibid.
68. Hopkins, *Being Human*, 128.
69. Ibid.
70. Ibid.
71. Ibid. Some other resources: Margaret Shih, Diana Sanchez, Courtney Bonam, and Courtney Peck, "The Social Construction of Race: Biracial Identity and Vulnerability," *Cultural Diversity and Ethnic Minority Psychology* 13, no. 2 (2007): 125–133.
72. Hopkins, *Being Human*, 128. Some other resources on the issue of white privilege: Paula S. Rothenberg, *White Privilege: Essential Readings on the Other Side of Racism, 2nd ed.* (New York, NY: Worth Publishing, 2004); Beverly Daniel Tatum, *Why Are All the Black Kids Sitting Together in the Cafeteria,* 5th Anniversary ed. (New York, NY: Basic Books, 2003); Cornel West, *Prophesy Deliverance: An Afro-American Revolutionary Christianity,* Anniversary ed. (Louisville, KY: John Knox Press, 2002).
73. Hopkins, *Being Human*, 129.
74. Because of the historical construction of race in the United States, some groups gravitate toward being white or are ascribed honorary whiteness. Asian Americans are an example of a group that is at times ascribed honorary whiteness. See http://asianamericanmovement.wordpress.

com/2010/03/27/76-of-asian-tras-considered-themselves-white/ (accessed December 2, 2013) for a description of the issue.

75. Hopkins, *Being Human*, 130.
76. Ibid., 131.
77. Ibid.
78. Andy Ostroy, "The Tea Party Movement Isn't about Racism? Read This...," huffingtonpost.com, April 15, 2010, http://www.huffing-tonpost.com/andy-ostroy/the-tea-party-, movement-is_b_538750.html (accessed October 17, 2013). According to Ostroy, "Contrary to how the movement is portrayed as a nonpartisan, multicultural, age/gender-diverse "big tent," most Tea Baggers are wealthy, white Republican males over 45, according to the poll. The poll chillingly illustrates what's really at the core of the movement: intense frustration, anger, and resent-ment over the belief that a black president is giving taxpayer handouts to other blacks. In fact, 25 percent believe the Obama administration favors blacks over whites. As the Times reports, they believe that "too much has been made of the problems facing black people."
79. Douglass, "The Present and Future of the Colored Race in America," 359.

## 3   Liberation for All

1. Barack Obama, "President's Obama Inaugural Address," January 21, 2013, http://www.usatoday.com/story/news/politics/2013/01/21/obama-inaugural-address/1851731/ (accessed February 14, 2013).
2. Martin Luther King, *A Testament of Hope: The Essential Writings and Speeches of Martin Luther King, Jr.*, James M. Washington, ed. (New York, NY: HarperCollins, 1991).
3. Ibid.
4. Kirsten West Savali, "Cornel West: President Obama Doesn't Deserve to Be Sworn in with MLK's Bible," *NewsOne: For Black America*, January 20, 2013, http://newsone.com/2153928/cornel-west-obama-mlk/ (accessed December 2, 2013).
5. Ibid.
6. Sean Sullivan, "How Republicans Have Attacked Obama's Inaugural Address, and What It Means," *The Washington Post*, January 25, 2013, http://www.washingtonpost.com/blogs/the-fix/wp/2013/01/25/how-republicans-have-attacked-obamas-inaugural-address-and-what-it-means/ (accessed December 2, 2013).
7. CNN Library, updated July 16, 2013 Trayvon Martin Shooting Fast Facts, http://www.cnn.com/2013/06/05/us/trayvon-martin-shooting-fast-facts (accessed July 22, 2013).
8. Ibid.
9. Ibid.
10. Ibid.

11. Ibid.
12. Ibid.
13. CBS/AP, "Outcry Unlikely to Spur Change in Stand-your-ground-law," July 21, 2013, http://www.cbsnews.com/8301–201_162–57594780/outcry-unlikely-to-spur-change-in-stand-your-ground-law/ (accessed July 22, 2013).
14. Julia Dahl, "Fla. Woman Marissa Alexander Gets 20 Years for "warning shot": Did She Stand Her Ground?" May 15, 2012, http://www.cbsnews.com/8301–504083_162–57434757–504083/fla-woman-marissa-alexander-gets-20-years-for-warning-shot-did-she-stand-her-ground/ (accessed July 22, 2013).
15. Ibid.
16. Ibid.
17. Ibid.
18. Ibid.
19. Ibid.
20. Ibid.
21. Ibid.
22. Ibid. The author discussed the exacerbating circumstances of Alexander violating parole and other factors that figured into the decision. Certainly these are important, but do not detract from the fact that she was denied the right to defend herself in the same manner as Zimmerman.
23. James H. Cone, *A Black Theology of Liberation*, Twentieth Anniversary Edition (Maryknoll, NY: Orbis Books, 1996), xvii.
24. By "not fitting" we mean they both had other issues that were exacerbating circumstances in their cases that rightly or wrongly influenced decisions.
25. Barack Obama, "Inaugural Address," http://www.whitehouse.gov/the-press-office/2013/01/21/inaugural-address-president-barack-obama (accessed July 23, 2013).
26. The title for this section is borrowed from Martin Luther King's book *Where Do We Go from Here: Chaos or Community?* (Boston: Beacon Press, 1967), 23–33
27. Ibid., 31.
28. Ibid., 33.
29. Ibid., 34.
30. Ibid., 35.
31. Ibid., 122.
32. Ibid.
33. Ibid.
34. Garth Kasimu Baker-Fletcher, *Xodus: An African American Male Journey* (Minneapolis, MN: Fortress Press, 1996), 107.
35. Ibid.
36. King, *Where Do We Go from Here?*, 122.
37. Ibid.
38. Baker-Fletcher, *Xodus*, 108.

39. King, *Where Do We Go from Here?*, 123.
40. Ibid.
41. Ibid., 25.
42. Ibid., 124.
43. Ibid.
44. James Cone, *God of the Oppressed* (San Francisco, CA: HarperCollins, 1975), 146.
45. Ibid., 147.
46. King, *Where Do We Go from Here?*, 125.
47. Ibid., 124.
48. Ibid., 126.
49. Ibid.
50. Ibid.
51. Ibid.
52. This is a term that Du Bois made prominent in 1905 when he wrote about it in *The Talented Tenth*.
53. Obama, "Inaugural Address," http://www.whitehouse.gov/the-press-office/2013/01/21/inaugural-address-president-barack-obama (accessed July 29, 2013).
54. Ibid.
55. Ibid.
56. Ibid.
57. Ibid.
58. Ibid.
59. Ibid.
60. Ibid.
61. Savali, "Cornel West."
62. Ibid.
63. NIV
64. Cone, *A Black Theology*, 85.
65. Ibid., 84–85.
66. Ibid., 85.
67. Ibid., 86.
68. Ibid., 87.
69. Ibid., 103.
70. Ibid.
71. Cone, *God of the Oppressed*, 147.
72. Ibid., 145.
73. Ibid., 146.
74. Ibid., 140.
75. Transcript of President Obama's speech after the George Zimmerman verdict, http://nbcpolitics.nbcnews.com/_news/2013/07/19/19564969-transcript-president-obamas-remarks-on-trayvon-martin-and-race?lite (accessed August 7, 2013)
76. Ibid.

# 4    The World House: Reclaiming the Dream of Dr. King in the Age of Obama

1. Martin Luther King Jr. delivered the "I Have a Dream" speech on the steps of the Lincoln Memorial in Washington, DC, on August 28, 1963. President Abraham Lincoln read the Emancipation Proclamation on January 1, 1863.
2. Martin Luther King Jr., "Letter from Birmingham Jail," April 1963.
3. Martin Luther King Jr., "I've Been to the Mountaintop," April 3, 1968, Memphis, Tennessee. See also James Melvin Washington's *A Testament of Hope: The Essential Writings of Martin Luther King Jr.* (New York, NY: HarperOne, 2003).
4. Ibid.
5. Ibid.
6. Matthew 26:52, New International Version.
7. See Johnny Bernard Hill's *Prophetic Rage: A Postcolonial Theology of Liberation* (Grand Rapids, MI: Eerdmans Publishing Co., 2013); *The Theology of Martin Luther King Jr. and Desmond Mpilo Tutu* (New York, NY: Palgrave Macmillan, 2007); and *The First Black President: Barack Obama, Race, Politics and the American Dream* (New York, NY: Palgrave Macmillan, 2009).
8. The US Constitution, Preamble.
9. Ralph Ellison, "What America Would Be without Blacks," *Time Magazine*, April 6, 1970.
10. Emancipation Proclamation, issued by then President Abraham Lincoln, January 1, 1963.
11. Albert J. Raboteau, *Slave Religion: The "Invisible Institution" in the Antebellum South* (Oxford: Oxford University Press, 2004).
12. Charles Marsh, *God's Long Summer: Stories of Faith and Civil Rights* (Princeton, NJ: Princeton University Press, 2008).
13. King, "I Have a Dream" speech, August 28, 1963, Washington, DC.
14. Ibid.
15. Ibid.

# 5    When Black Is Not Black Enough

1. For a biographical sketch of Martin and Malcolm see Cone's *Martin and Malcolm.* We differentiate between Martin black and Malcolm black in these ways. (1) Popular sentiment that Martin was more socially acceptable because of advocating for nonviolence. Malcolm was/is perceived by many as a hatemonger based on his rhetoric. For example, Malcolm's speech "God's Judgment on White America," (December 4, 1963) and his famous line of chickens coming home to roost is an example of this type of rhetoric. This type of rhetoric created

a perception that he stood for a different understanding of blackness than Martin. (2) Malcolm was/is perceived by many to be a separatist who did not want to coexist with African Americans. Martin was/is perceived to be an advocate for African Americans fitting into the American mainstream. To be Martin black is to buy into Anglo ideals and is perceived as fitting into the mainstream. To be Malcolm black is perceived as being against the mainstream and for a stronger black identity.

2. For more on why blackness continues to be an issue in America see *God and Race in American Politics* (Newark, NJ: Princeton University Press, 2008) by Mark Noll who argues that politics is a major factor in setting cultural norms (p. 14). Race is one of those norms. Also see Gregory D. Smithers and Clarence E. Walker, *The Preacher and the Politician: Jeremiah Wright, Barack Obama, and Race in America* (Charlottesville, VA: University of Virginia Press, 2009).

3. This example is controversial because of innuendos that Farrakhan had something to do with Malcolm's death. This connection also reflects a nonnuanced understanding of Malcolm's later positions.

4. Andrew Young was a colleague of King and eventual mayor of Atlanta. Kweisi Mfume is a former president of the NAACP.

5. Seth Gitell, "Is Obama Like King." http://www.nysun.com/opinion/is-obama-like-king/69072/ (accessed October 15, 2013).

6. Sharon Begley, "Why the Belief That Obama Is Muslim?" http://www.newsweek.com/2010/08/31/why-the-belief-that-obama-is-muslim.html (accessed October 15, 2013).

7. See James Cone, *God of the Oppressed* (San Francisco, CA: HarperCollins Publishing, 1975), 221 for how Du Bois's double-consciousness is perceived by some to be a part of African American fabric; see also Dwight Hopkins, *Introduction to Black Theology* (New York: Orbis Books, 1999), 5.

8. W. E. B. Du Bois, *The Souls of Black Folk*, Eric J. Sundquist, ed. (Oxford: Oxford University Press, 1966), 102.

9. In footnote six we pointed out those supporting an understanding of two-ness as a dichotomy, but Alton Pollard reads Du Bois differently.

10. One example is Victor Anderson's work. See *Beyond Ontological Blackness: An Essay on African American Religious and Cultural Criticism* (New York, NY: Continuum, 1995) and *Creative Exchange: A Constructive Theology of African American Religious Experience* (Minneapolis, MN: Fortress, 2008).

11. The Pew Forum reports are one example of studies on black religiosity.

12. This is one way of understanding the debate between Washington and Du Bois, King and Malcolm X, etc. The issue is when does one move beyond prophetic rhetoric to simply supporting an African American agenda. Prophetic rhetoric is perceived as aiding African Americans to fit (accommodate) into society. Nationalism is perceived as seeking to

destroy Anglo society for a new African American society. These posi-
tions are polarities and are often put into conversation with one another.
See Jacqueline M. Moore, Booker T. Washington, and W. E. B. Du Bois,
*The Struggle for Racial Uplift.*

13. Rev. Jeremiah Wright, who focused his ministry effort on the tenets
of Black Liberation Theology, is the Pastor Emeritus of Trinity United
Church of Christ where he was the senior pastor for 36 years.

14. Robert Tabscott, "The Media and the Rev. Wright," *St. Louis
Journalism Review*, July–August 2008, 38 no. 307 http://www.questia.
com/read/1G1–181714653 (accessed December 2, 2013).

15. Sonya Covet, Associated Content (Yahoo), "Barack Obama's Pastor,
Jeremiah Wright is a Racist: Why Are You Not More Outraged" associated content.com, March 18, 2008, http://voices.yahoo.com/barack-
obamas-pastor-jeremiah-wright-racist-1301127.html (accessed October
15, 2013).

16. Ibid.

17. Bill Moyers, *Journal*, April 25, 2008, http://www.pbs.org/moyers/
journal/04252008/transcript1.html (accessed October 15, 2013).

18. Ibid.

19. Covet.

20. Tavis Smiley is a radio host, author, and political commentator. Smiley
travels the country seeking to promote a stronger African American
community.

21. Al Sharpton is an ordained minister who is a social and political
activist.

22. We define blackness outside the parameters of a discussion about how
it affects the racial designation of those from the African Diaspora who
live in the United States.

23. Denise Stewart, "Smiley, Sharpton Spar Over Black Agenda, Obama,"
February 24, 2010, http://tlcnaptown.com/92381/smiley-sharpton-spar-
over-black-agenda-obama/ (accessed October 15, 2013).

24. One example is the public debate between Du Bois and Washington.
Powe recognizes that many perceive their disagreement as an issue
over blackness. Recent scholarship nuances their disagreement in some
important ways, but parallels can be drawn between their public wran-
gling and that of Smiley and Sharpton.

25. Certainly there is more to African American music than the lens we are
using, but it gives us insight into the particular part of black culture we
address in this chapter.

26. The term "sellout" is used in the public arena to describe someone who
receives status and it is believed this status is achieved because of Anglo
support. To read more on this term, see Ashley Pettus, "The 'Sellout,'"
*Harvard Magazine*, November/December 2007.

27. The idea of making black music is a perception. For example, The
Roots "The anti-circle," is about not giving into cultural norms and

maintaining a strong black presence. Eryka Badu's "Bag Lady," is about issues with which African American women contend. The perception of Will Smith's "Parents Just Don't Understand" is that it seeks to be a crossover tune that appeals to all. Our point is not that a logic exists in determining what is black or not, but that it is a reality in African American culture.

28. Ewuare X. Osayande, "An Open Letter to Will Smith about Denying Racism," Davey D's Daily Hip Hop News, February 5, 2009, http://hiphopnews.yuku.com/topic/1037 (accessed October 15, 2013).
29. Whitney Teal, "Who Gets to Define "Sell-out"? M.I.A. Meets the New York Times," Race in America, http://ontd-feminism.livejournal.com/165560.html?page=2 (accessed October 15, 2013).
30. For more on the history of this term, see www.asante.net (accessed October 15, 2013).
31. Ralph C. Watkins, "The Re-Radicalization of Black Theology: From Cone to Kemet," The A.M.E. Review 124, no. 416 (October/December 2009): 46.
32. Ibid., 50.
33. Brian Stelter, "A Dispute Over Obama's Birth Lives on in the Media," New York Times, July 24, 2009, http://www.nytimes.com/2009/07/25/business/media/25birther.html (accessed October 15, 2013).
34. James Cone, "The Marty Forum," American Academy of Religion, Montreal, Canada, November 8, 2009.
35. James Cone, Martin & Malcolm & America: A Dream or a Nightmare (Maryknoll, NY: Orbis Books, 1993), 247.
36. Ibid., 270.
37. Sean Hannity, "IObama's Pastor: Reverent Jeremiah Wright," March 2, 2007, http://www.foxnews.com/story/2007/03/02/obama-pastor-rev-jeremiah-wright/ (accessed October 15, 2013).
38. Ibid.
39. Ibid.
40. Ibid.
41. Cone, Martin & Malcolm, 64.
42. Ibid., 67.
43. Ibid.
44. Ibid., 93.
45. Ibid.
46. Ibid., 96.
47. Ibid., 100.
48. Ibid.
49. Ibid., 102; also see The Eyes on the Prize PBS series for those perceiving Malcolm as a prophet of hate, http://www.pbs.org/wgbh/amex/eyesontheprize/ (accessed October 15, 2013).
50. Ibid., 103
51. Ibid.

52. Ibid.
53. Obama's slogan "Yes WE Can!" The we includes all United States citizens.
54. Ibid., 246.
55. Ibid.
56. James Cone, *A Black Theology of Liberation* (Maryknoll, NY: Orbis Books, 1994), 15.
57. James Cone, *A Black Theology of Liberation*, 120.
58. Ibid., 122.
59. Ibid., 113.
60. Cecil Cone, *The Identity Crisis in Black Theology* (Nashville: AMEC, 1975), 22–23.
61. Karen Baker-Fletcher, *Dancing with God: The Trinity from a Womanist Perspective* (St. Louis, MO: Chalice Press, 2006), 49.
62. Ibid., 46.
63. Ibid., 45–46.
64. Ibid., 56.
65. Ibid.
66. Ibid.
67. Ibid.
68. Ibid.
69. Obama's new controversial health-care policy. How does this policy truly affect those in the African American community? This is a different approach than simply saying we support Obama's policy because he is African American or we do not support it because he is not African enough.

# 6   Reclaiming the Prophetic: Toward a Theology of Hope and Justice in a Fragmented World

1. Peter J. Paris, "Unfinished Business," http://www.hds.harvard.edu/news-events/harvard-divinity-bulletin/articles/unfinished-business (accessed December 6, 2013).
2. Leonardo Boff, *Global Civilization: Challenges to Society and Christianity* (London: Equinox, 2003), 5.
3. Ibid.
4. Ibid.
5. Ibid.
6. Ibid., 1.
7. http://www.who.int/hdp/poverty/en/ (accessed October 17, 2013).
8. Examples in the United States include: the Jena Six incident involving six black youth in Jena, Louisiana, who were arrested and charged for

participating in a school yard fight with fellow white classmates; Henry Louis Gates' arrest at his home on the campus of Harvard University in 2010; and, regular (less notable) occurrences of police brutality and false arrests throughout the nation. In the global arena, ethnic tensions continue in the Balkans, Italy, and France, particularly among Jews, Christians, and Muslims. The rising Islamic populations in Europe have become a destabilizing narrative to Western identity as it heightens concerns over ethnic and religious intolerance.

9. David Walker, *Walker's Appeal*, published 1829. (Houston, TX: African Diaspora Press, 2013).

10. See Robert Edgar Conrad's *Children of God's Fire: A Documentary History of Black Slavery in Brazil* (Princeton, NJ: Princeton University Press, 1983); Herbert S. Klein, *African Slavery in Latin America and the Caribbean* (Oxford: Oxford University Press, 2007); Darien J. Davis, *Beyond Slavery: The Multilayered Legacy of Africans in Latin America and the Caribbean* (Memphis, TN: General Books, LLC, 2010).

11. Georg Wilhelm Friedrich Hegel, *The Philosophy of History* (New York, NY: Dover Publications, 1956).

12. Lawrence Cahoone, *From Modernism to Postmodernism: An Anthology* (Cambridge, MA: Blackwell, 1996), 11.

13. Martin Luther King Jr., *Where Do We Go from Here: Chaos or Community?* (Eugene, OR: Wipf and Stock, reprinted, 1991), 195.

14. James Cone, Remarks at the Black Religious Scholars Group Session, American Academy of Religion Meeting, October 2009, San Diego, CA.

15. Jim Wallis and Joyce Hollyday, ed., *Cloud of Witnesses* (Maryknoll, NY: Orbis Books, 2005). See also Elizabeth Castelli's *Martyrdom and Memory: Early Christian Culture Making* (New York, NY: Columbia University Press, 2004).

16. In recent memory, figures like Martin Luther King Jr. and Dietrich Bonhoeffer are individuals who were able to transcend their particular historical situations by directly engaging the political systems of their time. King, rooted in the American South, challenged Jim Crow segregation and later the Vietnam War, and the wider issue of poverty in the United States of America and globally. Dietrich Bonhoeffer was a leader in the underground movement to resist Adolf Hitler's Third Reich in Germany during World War II and the rise of Nazism.

17. Albert J. Raboteau, *Slave Religion: The "Invisible Institution" in the Antebellum South* (Oxford, London: Oxford University Press, 2004).

18. Johnny B. Hill, *The First Black President: Barack Obama, Race, Politics, and the American Dream* (New York, NY: Palgrave Macmillan, 2009).

19. Hill, *The First Black President*; See also Charles Villa-Vicencio, *A Theology of Reconstruction: Nation-Building and Human Rights* (Cambridge: Cambridge University Press, 1992). The Truth and Reconciliation Commission was an effort in South Africa after apartheid

to create a peaceful transition into a more democratic existence. The Commission itself was convened by Archbishop Desmond Tutu and invited victims (or families of deceased persons) and perpetrators to come and speak truth about what happened during apartheid. One of the challenges of the Commission is some families felt it let the perpetrators off the hook (e.g., the Steve Biko family).

20. Hill, *The First Black President*. See also Gwen Ifill, *The Breakthrough: Politics and Race in the Age of Obama* (New York, NY: Anchor Books, 2009); Paul Street, *Barack Obama and the Future of American Politics* (Boulder, CO: Paradigm Publishers, 2008).

21. The public schools that are struggling with accreditation issues are inner city. Kansas City and St. Louis, Missouri public schools are two examples of this struggle.

22. James Waller, *Face to Face: The Changing State of Racism across America* (Jackson, TN: Basic Books, 1998).

23. By "post-Civil Rights era," we refer to the period between roughly 1968 to the present, where the prominence and public influence of many historic Civil Rights organizations (Southern Christian Leadership Conference (SCLC), Congress of Racial Equality (CORE), Student Nonviolent Coordinating Committee (SNCC)) have witnessed a gradual decline. It is also an era where modes of black political activism and political mobilization chiefly take the form of electoral politics in local and national elections.

24. Molefi Kete Asanti, *The Afrocentric Idea* (Philadelphia, PA: Temple University Press, 1998) and *Afrocentricity* (Chicago, IL: Africa World Press, 2003); Randall Robinson, *The Debt: What America Owes to Blacks* (New York, NY: Plume Publishers, 2001).

25. W. E. B. Du Bois, *The Souls of Black Folks*, published 1903 (New York, NY: Penguin Classics, 1996).

26. Kevin Kelly Gaines, *Uplifting the Race: Black Leadership, Politics and Culture in the Twentieth Century* (North Carolina: University of North Carolina Press, 1996).

27. Johann Wolfgang von Goethe (1749–1832), http://www.great-quotes.com/quote/1359782 (accessed April 27, 2013).

28. By "black community," we mean the collective social, political, and cultural life of black people (or African Americans) in America, which includes the multiple dimensions of black identity (Afro-latinos, Caribbeans, African immigrants, and others who identify with the historical struggle of black resistance to systemic racism in the nation).

29. Mary Pattillo, *Black on the Block: The Politics of Race and Class in the City* (Chicago, IL: University of Chicago Press, 2007).

30. Ibid.

31. Eboo Patel is founder of the Interfaith Youth Core, based in Chicago, Illinois. The organization seeks to increase awareness of faith traditions, promoting interfaith dialogue, mutual understanding, and tolerance. It

focuses on youth development by bringing together youth from different faith traditions to perform social justice and community projects. Patel is also author of *Acts of Faith: The Story of An American Muslim, the Struggle for the Soul of a Generation* (Boston, MA: Beacon Press, 2007).

32. Michelle Alexander, *The New Jim Crow: Mass Incarceration in an Age of Colorblindness* (New York, NY: New Press, 2010).

33. Ibid.

34. Some of the critics of liberation theologies in recent years have been the Radical Orthodoxy school of thought that includes such thinkers as Graham Ward, Kathyrn Pickstock, and John Milbank. J. Kameron Carter's book, *Race: A Theological Account*, is another example of recent assaults on liberation theologies, which reinforce Western epistemologies and intellectual systems of knowledge and political power. These critiques should be looked upon as suspect because they do not seem to emerge from within the discourse on liberation theologies among those theologians in the tradition representing an ongoing dialogue for more than half a century.

35. Thomas Aquinas, edited by Timothy McDermott, *Summa Theologiae* (New York, NY: Christian Classics, 1991).

36. Hugo Rahner, *Church and State in Early Christianity* (New York, NY: Ignatius Press, 2006).

37. René Descartes, *The Cambridge Companion to Descartes* (Cambridge: Cambridge University Press, 1992).

38. Hegel, *Philosophy of History.*

39. Martin Luther King Jr., *Letter from Birmingham Jail* (New York, NY: HarperCollins Publishers, 1994).

40. Robert McAfee Brown, ed., *Kairos: Three Prophetic Challenges to the Church* (Grand Rapids, MI: William B. Eerdmans, 1990), 2.

41. Karl Barth, "The Barmen Declaration," written 1934, in *Kairos: Three Prophetic Challenges to the Church.*

42. *Kairos: Challenge to the Church,* written in the Explanatory notes in *Kairos: Three Prophetic Challenges to the Church.*

43. *Kairos Central America,* Para. 86 in *Kairos: Three Prophetic Challenges to the Church.*

44. *Road To Damascus,* Para. 86, in *Kairos: Three Prophetic Challenges to the Church.*

45. Brown, *Kairos: Three Prophetic Challenges to the Church,* 7.

46. James Cone, *A Black Theology of Liberation* (Maryknoll, NY: Orbis Books, 1972); Gustavo Gutierrez, *Liberation Theology* (Maryknoll, NY: Orbis Books, 1969). Jacquelyn Grant, Katie Geneva Cannon, and Delores Williams, in particular, are among the pioneering womanist religious scholars who highlighted the experience of black women within a broader struggle for black freedom and dignity. Rosemary Ruether and Letty Russell, though sympathetic to the Womanist cause, are grounded

in feminist theological discourse, yet contribute greatly to the field of liberation theology in general. Leonardo Boff, like Gutierrez, comes out of the Latin American context.

47. It is important to note that the "Christian tradition" is comprised multiple histories, perspectives, languages, cultural contexts, and theologies. For instance, Greek Orthodox, Ethiopian Orthodox, Catholic, and Protestant traditions (which make up their own unique subsets) are merely some of the various communities within the larger Christian tradition originating in first-century Palestine.

48. J. Deotis Roberts, *Liberation and Reconciliation* (Maryknoll, NY: Orbis books), 84.

49. Albrecht Ritschl, edited by Hugh Ross Mackintosh and Alexander Beith Macaulay, *The Christian Doctrine of Justification and Reconciliation* (Whitefish, MT: Kessinger Publishing, 2006)

50. See Michael Battle's *Reconciliation: The Ubuntu Theology of Desmond Mpilo Tutu* (Cleveland, OH: Pilgrim Press, 1997).

51. Ibid.

52. King, *Where Do We Go from Here?*, 222–223.

53. http://thinkexist.com/quotes/mother_teresa_of_calcutta/ (accessed July 25, 2013).

# 7   The World House: The Beloved Community as a New Global Vision for Peace and Justice

1. Taylor Branch, *Pillar of Fire: America in the King Years, 1963–65* (New York, NY: Simon and Schuster, 1998), xiii.

2. Martin Luther King Jr., *Where Do We Go from Here?: Chaos or Community?* (Boston, MA: Beacon Press, 1968).

3. Martin Luther King, Jr., *Where Do We Go from Here: Chaos or Community?* (Eugene, OR: Wipf and Stock Publishers, 2002; previously published by Harper and Row, Publishers, Inc. 1991), 195.

4. Martin Luther King, Jr., "Letter from Birmingham Jail," April 16, 1963.

5. Elizabeth Moltmann Wendel and Jurgen Moltmann, *Humanity in God* (New York, NY: The Pilgrim Press, 1983), 63.

6. Kwok Pui-lan, Don H. Compier, and Joerg Rieger, eds., *Empire and the Christian Tradition: New Readings of Classical Theologians* (Minneapolis, MN: Fortress, 2007), 10.

7. Michael Hardt and Antonio Negri, *Empire* (Cambridge, MA: Harvard University Press, 2000), xii. See also Kwon Pui-lan's "Theology and Social Theory" in *Empire and the Christian Tradition*, 23.

8. Pui-lan, Compier, Rieger, eds., *Empire and the Christian Tradition*, 23.

9. James Melvin Washington, ed., *A Testament of Hope: Selected Writings of Martin Luther King Jr.* (New York, NY: HarperOne Publishers, 1990). The text is a compilation of King's sermons, articles, essays, and interviews throughout his time as a public leader in the civil rights movement.

10. Noel L. Erskine, 1994, *King Among the Theologians* (Cleveland, OH: Pilgrim Press, 1995), 47.

11. Martin Luther King, Jr., 1948, "A Comparison of the Conceptions of God in the Thinking of Paul Tillich and Henry Nelson Wieman," Dissertation from Boston University Graduate School, submitted in partial fulfillment of the requirements for the degree of Doctor of Philosophy.

12. Erskine, *King Among the Theologians*, 47.

13. King, *Where Do We Go from Here?*, 179.

14. Ibid., 194.

15. King, "Nobel Prize Acceptance Speech," in *A Testament of Hope: The Essential Writings of Martin Luther King, Jr.*, James M. Washington, ed. (New York, NY: HarperSanFrancisco, 1988), 224.

16. David J. Garrow, *Bearing the Cross: Martin Luther King, Jr., and the Southern Christian Leadership Conference* (New York, NY: Vintage Books, 1988), 431.

17. James M. Washington, ed., *A Testament of Hope: The Essential Writings and Speeches of Martin Luther King, Jr.* (New York, NY: HarperSanFrancisco, 1988), 189.

18. Garrow, *Bearing the Cross*, 551.

19. King, *Where Do We Go from Here?*, 195.

20. Ibid., 196.

21. Ibid., 200.

22. Ibid., 202.

23. Cf. King's *Where Do We Go from Here?: Chaos or Community?* (Boston, MA: Beacon Press, 1968).

24. Johnny B. Hill, *The Theology of Martin Luther King, Jr. and Desmond Mpilo Tutu* (New York, NY: Palgrave Macmillan Press, 2007).

25. King, *Where Do We Go from Here?*

26. Gianni Vattimo, *The End of Modernity: Nihilism and Hermeneutics in Postmodern Culture* (Baltimore, MD: Johns Hopkins University Press, 1991).

27. Jeffrey Sachs, *The End of Poverty: Economic Possibilities for Our Time* (New York: Penguin, 2005), 5–25.

28. Washington, *A Testament of Hope*, 130.

29. Martin Luther King Jr., Selma Speech, March 25, 1965, Montgomery, Alabama.

30. Ibid.

31. Ibid.

32. Ibid.

33. King, "Cradle of the Confederacy" Speech, 1965, Selma, Alabama.
34. Taylor Branch, *At Canaan's Edge: America in the King Years 1965–1968* (New York, NY: Simon and Schuster, 2006), 684.
35. King, "I've Been to the Mountain Top," Speech, April 3, 1968, Mason Temple, (Church of God in Christ Headquarters) Memphis, Tennessee.

# 8   Unlocking Doors of Hope: A Quest for Enduring Peace and Justice

1. Martin Luther King Jr. "I Have a Dream" speech delivered on March 1963 in Washington, http://www.archives.gov/press/exhibits/dream-speech.pdf (accessed August 9, 2013).
2. Dr. Ralph Bunche, United Nations Ambassador, received the 1950 Nobel Peace Prize for "his successful mediation of a series of armistice agreements between the new nation of Israel and four Arab neighbors, Egypt, Jordan, Lebanon and Syria." See http://www.nobelprize.org /nobel_prizes/peace/laureates/1950/bunche-bio.html and http://www .pbs.org/ralphbunche/peace_nobel.html (accessed August 9, 2013). South African Chief Albert Luthuli was awarded the prize in 1960 for his role in the anti-Apartheid struggle http://www.nobelprize.org/nobel_prizes /peace/laureates/1960/lutuli-bio.html and http://africanhistory.about. com/library/biographies/blbio-lutuli.htm (accessed August 9, 2013). For additional information, see David Levering Lewis, *King: A Biography*, 2nd edition (Urbana, IL: University of Illinois Press, 1978), 255; Stephen B. Oates, *Let the Trumpet Sound: A Life of Martin Luther King, Jr.* (New York, NY: Harper Perennial, 1994), 312; David J. Garrow, *Bearing the Cross: Martin Luther King, Jr., and the Southern Christian Leadership Conference* (New York: Vintage Books, 1988), 357.
3. Jeff Zeleny, "Accepting Peace Prize Will Be a Test for Obama," http: //www.nytimes.com/2009/12/09/us/politics/09prize.html?_r=0 (accessed March 15, 2013). In preparation for his Nobel Lecture, Zeleny shares the following about President Obama: "A student of history, he read the lecture of Theodore Roosevelt, who won the award in 1906 for his role in bringing an end to the war between Russia and Japan. He also studied the words of Woodrow Wilson, who sent a telegram to the committee – he was ill and could not attend a ceremony – for his 1919 award in recognition of his 14-point peace program for ending World War I.
4. For an example of these entitlement programs which at their core are "affirmative action" initiatives but never designated as such, consider admission policies designed to accommodate family members of select alumni.
5. Congress shall make no law respecting an establishment of religion, or prohibiting the free exercise thereof; or abridging the freedom of speech, or of the press; or the right of the people peaceably to assemble, and

to petition the Government for a redress of grievances. http://constitu-tion.findlaw.com/amendment1/amendment.html (accessed September 4, 2013).

6. Martin Luther King Jr., Nobel Peace Prize Acceptance Speech in Oslo from *Les Prix Nobel en 1964*, Editory Göran Liljestrand, [Nobel Foundation], Stockholm, 1965, http://www.nobelprize.org/nobel _prizes/peace/laureates/1964/king-acceptance_en.html (accessed January 18, 2013).

7. In his acceptance lecture, Barack Obama noted the tension that was inherent with his dual role of president and commander in chief. Barack H. Obama – "A Just and Lasting Peace," Nobel Lecture. Nobelprize. org February 15, 2013, http://www.nobelprize.org/nobel_prizes/peace /laureates/2009/obama-lecture_en.html (accessed February 15, 2013).

8. David Remnick, *The Bridge: The Life and Rise of Barack Obama* (New York: Alfred A. Knopf, 2010), 583.

9. For analysis of Barack Obama's application of just war theory see: Kelly Denton-Borhaug, "Beyond Iraq and Afghanistan: Religion and Politics in United States War-Culture," *Dialog: A Journal of Theology* 51, no. 2 (June 2012); William F. Felice, "President Obama's Nobel Peace Prize Speech: Embracing the Ethics of Reinhold Niebuhr." *Social Justice* 37, nos. 2–3 (2010–2011); Juan M. Floyd-Thomas, "More Than Conquerors: Just War Theory and the Need for a Black Christian Antiwar Movement." *Black Theology* 9, no. 2 (August 1, 2011): 136–160; Chris Herlinger, "Obama's Peace Prize Speech Explores the Ethics of Warfare." *Christian Century* (January 12, 2010): 13–14; David Krieger, "The Nobel War Lecture." *National Catholic Reporter* 46, no. 6 (January 8, 2010): 24; Cian O'Driscoll, "Talking about Just War: Obama in Oslo, Bush at War." *Politics* 31, no. 2 (June 2011): 82–90.

10. Harlem Renaissance poet Langston Hughes posed this thought provok-ing question in his classic poem, "A Dream Deferred" perhaps as a way to encourage informed responses to multiple injustices that character-ized life in the United States during the era known as Jim Crow.

11. See then Senator Obama's January 2008 New Hampshire concession speech    http://politics.nuvvo.com/lesson/4678-transcript-of-obamas-speech-yes-we-can (accessed September 17, 2013).

12. King, Nobel Peace Prize Acceptance Speech.

13. Kent B. Germany, "War on Poverty," http://faculty.virginia.edu/sixties /readings/War%20on%20Poverty%20entry%20Poverty%20 Encyclopedia.pdf (accessed September 17, 2013).

14. Brandon James Smith, "A Better War on Poverty; Free Enterprise Empowers Individuals to Become Achievers," *The Washington Times* (Washington, DC), June 25, 2013, http://www.questia.com /read/1G1–334943022.

15. For additional information on the War on Poverty, see: Robert Higgs, "The Great Society's War on Poverty," *Freeman*, October 2011,

http://www.questia.com/read/1P3-2475464131;    Nicole    Kenney, "Economic Snapshot: The Social Safety Net and Its Impact on Poverty," *The Crisis*, Spring 2012, 47, http://www.questia.com/read/1P3- 2898471001; Bruce D. Meyer and James X. Sullivan, "Winning the War: Poverty from the Great Society to the Great Recession," *Brookings Papers on Economic Activity*, 2012, http://www.questia.com/read/1G1 -327585902; Ted Nugent, "War on Poverty Is Over – We Lost; Nearly 50 Years and $15 Trillion Later, the Poor Are Still Poor," *The Washington Times* (Washington, DC), April 24, 2012, http://www.questia.com/ read/1G1-287507350; Frank Stricker, Why America Lost the War on Poverty – and How to Win It (Chapel Hill, NC: University of North Carolina Press, 2007); Michael Tanner, "The 15 Trillion Dollar War on Poverty Is a Failure," *USA TODAY*, September 2012, http://www .questia.com/read/1G1-303071865; Tonyaa Weathersbee, "Fight War on Poverty, Not on the Poor," *The Florida Times Union*, January 12, 2012, http://www.questia.com/read/1G1-279298070. For War on Drugs, see: Michael Keane, "A Roadmap to Peace in the War on Drugs," *Review – Institute of Public Affairs*, October 2012, http://www.questia. com/read/1P3-2876314071; Joseph D. McNamara, "The Hidden Costs of America's War on Drugs." *Journal of Private Enterprise* 26, no. 2 (2011), http://www.questia.com/read/1P3-2371417441; Doris Marie Provine, *Unequal under Law: Race in the War on Drugs* (Chicago, IL: University of Chicago Press, 2007); Daniel Williams, "The War on Drugs," *Contemporary Review*, September 2012, http://www.questia. com/read/1G1-307673846.

16. See http://datacenter.kidscount.org/data/tables/43-children-in-poverty? loc=1&loct=1#detailed/1/any/false/868,867,133,38,35/any/321,322 (accessed September 18, 2013).

17. John 12.8 and Matthew 26.11 (NRSV).

18. Mark 14.7b (NRSV).

19. Supposedly designed to minimize residential foreclosures, the law did not mandate that lenders work with borrowers to refinance mortgages. As a result, bank profits increased as home foreclosures soared. For information on the 2008 Housing and Economic Recovery Act, see Viral V. Acharya et al., *Guaranteed to Fail: Fannie Mae, Freddie Mac, and the Debacle of Mortgage Finance* (Princeton, NJ: Princeton University Press, 2011); Thomas H. Stanton, *Why Some Firms Thrive While Others Fail: Governance and Management Lessons from the Crisis* (New York, NY: Oxford University Press, 2012); http://www.hud.gov/news/recov- eryactfaq.cfm (accessed December 7, 2013); https://www.govtrack.us /congress/bills/110/hr3221 (accessed December 7, 2013).

20. See http://www.ontheissues.org/celeb/Bill_Clinton_Welfare_+_Poverty .htm (accessed September 18, 2013).

21. Peter Edelman, "The Worst Thing Bill Clinton Has Done," in The Atlantic Monthly Digital Edition, March 1997, http://www.theatlantic.

com/past/docs/issues/97mar/edelman/edelman.htm (accessed October 21, 2013).

22. Martin Luther King Jr., "The Quest for Peace and Justice," Nobel Lecture, December 11, 1964 from *Les Prix Nobel en 1964* Editory Göran Liljestrand, [Nobel Foundation], Stockholm, 1965, http://www.nobelprize.org/nobel_prizes/peace/laureates/1964/king-lecture.html (accessed January 18, 2013).

23. Ibid.

24. ASPE Human Services Policy Staff, "Information on Poverty and Income Statistics: A Summary of 2012 Current Population Survey Data," September 12, 2012 http://aspe.hhs.gov/hsp/12/povertyandincomeest/ib.shtml (accessed 21 September 2013).

25. See David Rogers, "House GOP Seeks Cuts in Food Stamps," *Politico*, September 16, 2013, http://www.politico.com/story/2013/09/house-gop-seeks-tighter-food-stamp-rules-96873.html accessed October 21, 2013.

26. Jon Healey, "Federal Debt Still a Problem, But So Is Poverty," *Los Angeles Times*, September 17, 2013, http://articles.latimes.com/2013/sep/17/news/la-ol-federal-debt-problem-poverty-20130917 (accessed October 21, 2013).

27. Democracy Now!, "So Rich, So Poor": Peter Edelman on Ending U.S. Poverty & Why He Left Clinton Admin over Welfare Law," May 23, 2012 http://www.democracynow.org/2012/5/23/so_rich_so_poor_peter_edelman (accessed October 21, 2013).

28. King, "The Quest for Peace and Justice."

29. King, Nobel Peace Prize Acceptance Speech.

30. King, "The Quest for Peace and Justice."

31. Ibid.

32. "I Shall Not Be Moved," words by Edward H. Boatner, http://www.pdhymns.com/SheetMusic/I-Q/I_SheetMusic/I%20Shall%20Not%20Be%20Moved.pdf (accessed October 21, 2013).

33. King, "The Quest for Peace and Justice."

34. Ibid.

35. Nicholas Wolterstorff, "For Justice in Shalom," in *From Christ to the World: Introductory Readings in Christian Ethics*, Wayne G. Boulton, Thomas D. Kennedy, and Allen Verhey, eds. (Grand Rapids, MI: William B. Eerdmans, 1994), 251.

36. Ibid.

37. Martin Luther King Jr. Nobel Peace Prize Acceptance Speech.

38. Ibid.

39. Ibid.

40. King, "The Quest for Peace and Justice,"

41. Ibid.

42. Angela D. Sims proposes we use this term to denote US citizens as one way to refute notions associated with an egalitarian assumption that does not recognize the vastness of the Americas.

43. Martin Luther King, Jr., "I Have a Dream," http://www.archives.gov/press/exhibits/dream-speech.pdf (accessed October 21, 2013).

44. King, "The Quest for Peace and Justice."

45. See "The Lack of Natural Born Citizen Status of Barack Hussein Obama, II," http://birthers.org (accessed October 21, 2013).

46. "FACT SHEET: The Affordable Care Act: Secure Health Coverage for the Middle Class," http://www.whitehouse.gov/the-press-office/2012/06/28/fact-sheet-affordable-care-act-secure-health-coverage-middle-class (accessed October 21, 2013).

47. Ibid.

48. Ibid.

49. Ibid.

50. Obama, "A Just and Lasting Peace."

51. Ibid.

52. 1 Corinthians 13.1b NRSV.

53. Obama, "A Just and Lasting Peace."

54. King, "The Quest for Peace and Justice."

# 9 Conclusion

1. Jini Kilgore Ross, ed., *What Makes You So Strong?: Sermons of Joy and Strength from Jeremiah A. Wright, Jr.* (Valley Forge: Judson, 1993), 98.

2. Ibid., 105.

# Bibliography

Alexander, Michelle. *The New Jim Crow: Mass Incarceration in an Age of Colorblindness*. New York, NY: New Press, 2010.

Anderson, Victor. *Beyond Ontological Blackness: An Essay on African American Religious and Cultural Criticism*. New York, NY: Continuum, 1995.

———. *Creative Exchange: A Constructive Theology of African American Religious Experience*. Minneapolis, MN: Fortress, 2008.

Asanti, Molefi Kete. *The Afrocentric Idea*. Philadelphia, PA: Temple University Press, 1998.

———. *Afrocentricity*. Chicago, IL: Africa World Press, 2003.

Baker-Fletcher, Karen. *Dancing with God: The Trinity from a Womanist Perspective*. St. Louis, MO: Chalice, 2006.

Baldwin, Lewis. "The Unfolding of the Moral Order: Rufus Burrow, Jr., Personal Idealism, and the Life and Thought of Martin Luther King, Jr." *Pluralist* 6, no. 1 (Spring 2011): 1–13.

———. *The Voice of Conscience: The Church in the Mind of Martin Luther King, Jr*. New York, NY: Oxford University Press, 2010.

Barone, Dennis. "James Logan and Gilbert Tennent: Enlightened Classicist Versus Awakened Evangelist." *Early American Literature* 21 (1986): 103–117.

Beecher, William C. and Rev. Samuel Scoville, assisted by Mrs. Henry Ward Beecher. *A Biography of Rev. Henry Ward Beecher*. New York, NY: Charles L. Webster & Company, 1888.

Benwell, Bethan and Elizabeth Stoke. *Discourse and Identity*. Edinburgh: Edinburgh University Press, 2007.

Boff, Leonardo. *Global Civilization: Challenges to Society and Christianity*. London: Equinox, 2003.

Branch, Taylor. *At Canaan's Edge: America in the King Years 1965–1968*. New York, NY: Simon and Schuster, 2006.

———. *Pillar of Fire: America in the King Years, 1963–65*. New York, NY: Simon and Schuster, 1998.

Branch, Taylor. Brueggemann, Walter. "Biblical Authority." In *Moral Issues & Christian Responses*, 8th ed. edited by Patricia Beattie Jung and L. Shannon Jung, 18–24. Minneapolis, MN: Fortress, 2012.

Burrow Jr., Rufus. "The Beloved Community: Martin Luther King, Jr. and Josiah Royce." *Encounter* 73, no. 1 (Fall 2012): 37–64.

Caldas-Coulthard, Carmen Rosa and Malcolm Coulthard, eds. *Texts and Practices: Readings in Critical Discourse Analysis*. London: Routledge, 1996.

Carter, J. Kameron. *Race: A Theological Account*. New York, NY: Oxford University Press, 2008.

Castelli, Elizabeth. *Martyrdom and Memory Early Christian Culture Making*. New York, NY: Columbia University Press, 2004.

Chesebrough, David B. *Charles G. Finney: Revivalistic Rhetoric*. Westport, CT: Greenwood Press, 2002.

Clark, Clifford E., Jr. *Henry Ward Beecher: Spokesman for a Middle-Class America*. Urbana, IL: University of Illinois Press, 1978.

Cone, James H. *A Black Theology of Liberation, 2nd ed.* Maryknoll, NY: Orbis, 1996.

Decker, Frank. "Working as a Team: Henry Ward Beecher and the Plymouth Congregation in the Anti-Slavery Cause." *International Congregational Journal* 8, no. 2 (Fall 2009): 33–42.

Delfino, Susan and Michele Gillespie, eds. *Neither Lady nor Slave: Working Women of the Old South*. Chapel Hill, NC: University of North Carolina Press, 2002.

Douglas, Kelly Brown. *Sexuality and the Black Church: A Womanist Perspective*. Maryknoll, NY: Orbis, 1999.

Erskine, Noel Leo and Bernice A. King. *King among the Theologians*. Cleveland, OH: Pilgrim, 1995.

Evensen, Bruce J. *God's Man for the Gilded Age: D. L. Moody and the Rise of Modern Mass Evangelism*. New York, NY: Oxford University Press, 2003.

Fairclough, Norman. *Analysing Discourse: Textual Analysis for Social Research*. London: Routledge, 2003.

Findlay, James F., Jr. *Dwight L. Moody: American Evangelists 1837–1899*. Chicago, IL: The University of Chicago Press, 1969.

Fishburn, Janet F. "Gilbert Tennent, Established "Dissenter."" *Church History* 63 (1994): 31–49.

Gaines, Kevin Kelly. *Uplifting the Race: Black Leadership, Politics and Culture in the Twentieth Century*. North Carolina: University of North Carolina Press, 1996.

Garrow, David J. *Bearing the Cross: Martin Luther King, Jr., and the Southern Christian Leadership Conference*. New York, NY: Vintage Books, 1986.

Guth, Karen V. "Reconstructing Nonviolence: The Political Theology of Martin Luther King Jr. After Feminism and Womanism." *Journal of the Society of Christian Ethics* 32, no. 1 (Spring–Summer 2012): 75–92.

Hardt, Michael and Antonio Negri. *Empire*. Cambridge, MA: Harvard University Press, 2000.

Hill, Johnny Bernard. *The First Black President: Barack Obama, Race, Politics and the American Dream*. New York, NY: Palgrave Macmillan, 2009.

———. *The Theology of Martin Luther King Jr. and Desmond Mpilo Tutu*. New York, NY: Palgrave Macmillan, 2007.

Hinds, Jay-Paul. "The Prophet's Wish: A Freudian Interpretation of Martin Luther King's Dream." *Pastoral Psychology* 61, no. 4 (August 2012): 467–484.

Hopkins, Dwight N. *Being Human: Race, Culture and Religion*. Minneapolis, MN: Fortress Press, 2005.

Ifill, Gwen. *The Breakthrough: Politics and Race in the Age of Obama*. New York, NY: Anchor Books, 2009.

Irons, Charles F. *The Origins of Proslavery Christianity: White and Black Evangelicals in Colonial and Antebellum Virginia*. Chapel Hill, NC: University of North Carolina Press, 2008.

King Jr., Martin Luther. Nobel Peace Prize Acceptance Speech in Oslo from *Les Prix Nobel en 1964*, Editory Göran Liljestrand, [Nobel Foundation], Stockholm, 1965.

———. *A Testament of Hope: Essential Writings and Speeches of Martin Luther King, Jr*. Edited by James M. Washington. New York, NY: HarperCollins, 1986.

———. *Where Do We Go from Here: Chaos or Community?* Eugene, OR: Wipf and Stock, reprinted 1991.

LaRue, Cleophus J. "Two Ships Passing in the Night." In *What's the Matter with Preaching Today?*, edited by Mike Graves, 127–144. Louisville, KY: Westminster John Knox Press, 2004.

Lewis, David L. *King: A Biography, 2nd ed*. Urbana, IL: University of Illinois Press, 1978.

Lischer, Richard. *The Preacher King: Martin Luther King, Jr. and the Word that Moved America*. New York, NY: Oxford University Press, 1995.

Marsh, Charles. *God's Long Summer: Stories of Faith and Civil Rights*. Princeton, NY: Princeton University Press, 2008.

McLoughlin, William G., ed. *Lectures on Revivals of Religion by Charles Grandison Finney*. Cambridge, MA: The Belknap Press of Harvard University Press, 1960.

Noll, Mark. *God and Race in American Politics*. Newark, NJ: Princeton University Press, 2008.

Oates, Stephen B. *Let the Trumpet Sound: A Life of Martin Luther King, Jr*. New York, NY: HarperPerennial, 1994.

Obama, Barack H. "A Just and Lasting Peace." Nobel Lecture.

Patel, Eboo. *Acts of Faith: The Story of an American Muslim, the Struggle for the Soul of a Generation*. Boston, MA: Beacon, 2007.

Pattillo, Mary. *Black on the Block: The Politics of Race and Class in the City*. Chicago, IL: University of Chicago Press, 2007.

Perciaccante, Marianne. *Calling Down Fire: Charles Grandison Finney and Revivalism in Jefferson County, New York, 1800–1840*. Albany, NY: State University of New York Press, 2003.

Pinn, Anne H. and Anthony B. Pinn. *Introduction to Black Church History*. Minneapolis, MN: Fortress, 2001.

Provine, Doris Marie. *Unequal Under Law: Race in the War on Drugs*. Chicago, IL: University of Chicago Press, 2007.

Pui-lan, Kwok, Don H. Compier, and Joerg Rieger, eds. *Empire and the Christian Tradition: New Readings of Classical Theologians*. Minneapolis, MN: Fortress, 2007.

Raboteau, Albert J. *Slave Religion: The "Invisible Institution" in the Antebellum South*. New York, NY: Oxford University Press, 2004.

Remnick, David. *The Bridge: The Life and Rise of Barack Obama*. New York, NY: Alfred A. Knopf, 2010.

Robinson, Randall. *The Debt: What America Owes to Blacks*. New York, NY: Plume Publishers, 2001.

Ross, Jini Kilgore, ed. *What Makes You So Strong?: Sermons of Joy and Strength from Jeremiah A. Wright, Jr.* Valley Forge, PA: Judson, 1993.

Rothenberg, Paula S. *White Privilege: Essential Readings on the Other Side of Racism, 2nd ed.* New York, NY: Worth Publishing, 2004.

Rubin, Julius H. *Religious Melancholy and Protestant Experience in America*. New York, NY: Oxford University Press, 1994.

Shaw, Wayne. "The Plymouth Pulpit: Henry Ward Beecher's Slave Auction Block." *ATQ* 14, no. 4 (December 2000): 335–343.

Smithers, Gregory D. and Clarence E. Walker. *The Preacher and the Politician: Jeremiah Wright, Barack Obama, and Race in America*. Charlottesville, VA: University of Virginia Press, 2009.

Street, Paul. *Barack Obama and the Future of American Politics*. Boulder, CO: Paradigm Publishers, 2008.

Talbot, Mary. *Media Discourse: Representation and Interaction*. Edinburgh: Edinburgh University Press, 2007.

Tatum, Beverly Daniel. *Why Are All the Black Kids Sitting Together in the Cafeteria, 5th ed.* New York: NY: Basic Books, 2003.

Wallis, Jim and Joyce Hollyday, eds. *Cloud of Witnesses*. Maryknoll, NY: Orbis, 2005.

Watkins, Ralph C. "The Re-Radicalization of Black Theology: From Cone to Kemet." *The A.M.E. Church Review* 124, no. 416 (Oct–Dec 2009): 43–58.

West, Cornel. *Prophesy Deliverance: An Afro-American Revolutionary Christianity.* Louisville, KY: John Knox Press, 2002.

West, Traci C. *Disruptive Christian Ethics: When Racism and Women's Lives Matter.* Louisville, KY: Westminster John Knox, 2006.

Worthington, Bruce. "Martin Luther King Jr. as Identificatory Conglomerate." *Black Theology: An International Journal* 11, no 2 [2013]: 219–239.

# Index

Printed and bound in the United States of America